Gordon and Ronni Lamont ha͏͏ [...] they produce creative resourc͏͏ [...] books such as *Drama Toolkit* and *Children Aloud* – as well as http://www.assemblies.org.uk, the SPCK school assembly web site which Gordon edits and Ronni contributes to.

Individually, Ronni writes sermons as Vicar of St John the Evangelist, Bexley, and Gordon writes books on drama in education, such as *100 Ideas for Drama* and the *BBC Drama Handbook* (http://www.writer.org.uk). He also writes radio drama and runs a creative consultancy on work–life balance, communications, team building and other organizational issues (http://www.lamonts.org.uk).

In their other life, they have two children, Claire and Jim. Ronni leads occasional dance workshops and Gordon works for the BBC on schools web sites (http://www.bbc.co.uk/schools).

Their interest in this area started to formalize when Gordon led the BBC's Work Life Balance project for eight months, but they had plenty of experience to build on balancing busy vicarage lives and working hard to find time to 'be' both as individuals and as a couple.

Overcoming Common Problems Series

For a full list of titles please contact
Sheldon Press, Marylebone Road, London NW1 4DU

Antioxidants
Dr Robert Youngson

The Assertiveness Workbook
Joanna Gutmann

Beating the Comfort Trap
Dr Windy Dryden and Jack Gordon

Body Language
Allan Pease

Body Language in Relationships
David Cohen

Calm Down
Dr Paul Hauck

Cancer – A Family Affair
Neville Shone

The Cancer Guide for Men
Helen Beare and Neil Priddy

The Candida Diet Book
Karen Brody

Caring for Your Elderly Parent
Julia Burton-Jones

Cider Vinegar
Margaret Hills

Comfort for Depression
Janet Horwood

Considering Adoption?
Sarah Biggs

Coping Successfully with Hay Fever
Dr Robert Youngson

Coping Successfully with Pain
Neville Shone

Coping Successfully with Panic Attacks
Shirley Trickett

Coping Successfully with PMS
Karen Evennett

Coping Successfully with Prostate Problems
Rosy Reynolds

Coping Successfully with RSI
Maggie Black and Penny Gray

Coping Successfully with Your Hiatus Hernia
Dr Tom Smith

Coping Successfully with Your Irritable Bladder
Dr Jennifer Hunt

Coping Successfully with Your Irritable Bowel
Rosemary Nicol

Coping When Your Child Has Special Needs
Suzanne Askham

Coping with Anxiety and Depression
Shirley Trickett

Coping with Blushing
Dr Robert Edelmann

Coping with Bronchitis and Emphysema
Dr Tom Smith

Coping with Candida
Shirley Trickett

Coping with Chronic Fatigue
Trudie Chalder

Coping with Coeliac Disease
Karen Brody

Coping with Cystitis
Caroline Clayton

Coping with Depression and Elation
Dr Patrick McKeon

Coping with Eczema
Dr Robert Youngson

Coping with Endometriosis
Jo Mears

Coping with Epilepsy
Fiona Marshall and
Dr Pamela Crawford

Coping with Fibroids
Mary-Claire Mason

Coping with Gallstones
Dr Joan Gomez

Coping with Headaches and Migraine
Shirley Trickett

Coping with a Hernia
Dr David Delvin

Coping with Long-Term Illness
Barbara Baker

Coping with the Menopause
Janet Horwood

Coping with Psoriasis
Professor Ronald Marks

Coping with Rheumatism and Arthritis
Dr Robert Youngson

Overcoming Common Problems Series

Overcoming Common Problems Series

Overcoming Common Problems

WORK–LIFE BALANCE
Change the Way You Live With Work

Gordon and Ronni Lamont

sheldon PRESS

First published in Great Britain in 2001 by
Sheldon Press
Holy Trinity Church
Marylebone Road
London NW1 4DU

British Library Cataloguing-in-Publication Data
A catalogue record for this book is available from the British Library

ISBN 0–85969–848–3

Typeset by Deltatype, Birkenhead, Merseyside
Printed in Great Britain by Biddles Ltd
www.biddles.co.uk

Contents

For Josh, who made a difference

1
Your life in balance

What picture does the word 'balance' conjure up for you – scales of justice, a tightrope walker, or perhaps a healthy meal? Maybe you think of a more abstract notion such as the balance of nature or a balance of probabilities; it could be that you have a picture of serenity, calmness and things being 'just right'. However you picture it, balance is about dynamics and equilibrium – things that are active, like gravity or the ecosystem finding their right place in relation to other things and to each other. Balance is never static though it may be still; balance is always alive, poised, and responsive. Even that peaceful, balanced picture achieves its equilibrium by all the elements working together and against each other. Balanced systems are always ready to adjust and shift in order to maintain stability. The tree in your idyllic landscape is the shape it is because it has pushed up against gravity toward the light, so in one sense it is balanced between the sun and the earth; but it is alive and will change and develop in response to its environment and its own growth. The scales of justice weigh the evidence on both sides of an argument – a shifting, dynamic system again. Anything that you can think of that is 'in balance' will have a tension, a life, a power built into it. A truer phrase than 'in balance' would be 'held in balance' but it is not such a snappy title!

This book is about a balance that includes your work and the rest of your life. It's about understanding the creative tension of the work–life continuum, and making it work for you. We'll look at things that you can change

- within yourself;
- in your relationships;
- in the way that you work;
- in the structure of organizations;
- in others' expectations and responses.

This is not just about 'family-friendly' policies – these issues affect anyone who works. Although much of the recent driving force has come from parents, particularly those with young children and/or

1

elder care responsibilities, we see work and your relationship with it as part of who you are – whoever you are.

What do we mean by 'work'?

Let's try a few definitions. Work is:

- something you have to do;
- vocational;
- what you do to earn money;
- what you do that you don't want to do but it brings in the cash/ brings in the pennies/brings home the bacon/wins you the bread;
- work is what you do that you don't want to do and it doesn't bring in the cash/bring in the pennies/bring home the bacon/win you the bread;
- your reason for living;
- your defining activity;
- something to fill the time;
- wonderful;
- terrible;
- underpaid;
- overpaid – but don't tell anyone.

While we can say is that work has been with us right from the very beginning when Adam was told to subdue the land, it is clear that work now is multifaceted and varied. It is whatever it is for you. It might be paid, voluntary, forced or lovingly embraced. It might be work in the home (paid or unpaid), it might be childcare (ditto). Even within the formal structure of 'going to work' there are so many options and styles, from desk-based to out and about, from freelance to salaried. The range is enormous. Any single word that can encompass activities as diverse as shelling peas or flying into space is bound to have a pretty broad definition.

This gives us a problem because a book like this cannot hope to cover all the issues for all the different types of work that our readers will be engaged in. Instead we've attempted to focus on principles, issues and questions – the idea is to get you to do the work (while we get the royalty, of course!). We've tended to concentrate on the areas that we know – media, freelance work, clergy, office – and home-based professionals. We make no apology for narrowing the focus as we believe that many of the principles underpinning the book can be applied in many situations. For example, we don't deal explicitly with issues relating to unpaid housework and childcare (very real work–life balance areas for many of our readers), but we do talk about setting boundaries and making time for yourself in the context of working at home, and it's easy to see how the one area can inform the other.

Even so, we know that many jobs simply don't have the kind of flexibility that the examples in this book offer – you can't work at home if you're a logger and you can't work three days a week if this means you're unable to pay the bills. What you can do, in each of these cases, is step back and think about what you're doing. You can reassess where you're going in relation to work and you can think creatively about the when, where and how. Not all options will apply to all jobs but issues such as career breaks, lifelong learning and many others covered in the book will be relevant to many situations. This book can't make a difference – but perhaps, by using it, you can.

Beginning to think about the issues

There are books that touch on the strong business case for tailoring the nature and shape of work to suit the individual. We go into some of those arguments later in this book, but the key feature of what we have to say is that this is about *you* – about changes you can make to your approach, personal circumstances and in the nature of your working life. This book is about change.

Consider these statements. Do any describe your situation?

- I work too hard.
- After work I have too little energy for other important parts of my life.
- My work causes tension in my relationships.
- I don't feel like a whole person – my work causes an imbalance in my sense of self.
- My work isn't fulfilling.
- I don't have enough to do.
- I want a more challenging job.

- I'm letting my children down because of my work.
- I should get fitter, but there's no time.
- I keep putting off things I want to do.
- My life is too crowded.
- My work makes me angry.

If you can sign up to any of those statements, then perhaps there are things you could change in your work–life balance story. We hope that some of the ideas in this book will help you to shift the dynamic to bring more balance to your life. You probably won't be able to change everything that you'd like to, but you will be able to identify and work on some aspects, and our hope is that you will be able to bring about real change in how you live with work.

In order to change we need to understand where we are at present and where we wish to be, and we need to find a pathway from the one to the other. There will be parts of the path that we can tread ourselves, and other sections where we can make no progress without change and support from others. We will need to keep our destination in mind, but be flexible enough to modify how we plan to get there, and even to set different targets as we learn more about our real aims and ourselves.

There are guiding principles underlying the processes that this book aims to take you through:

- Understand where you are.
- Assess where you want to be.
- Apply the experience of others to your own situation.
- Identify what you can change.
- Take action.

Sounds simple, doesn't it? Here's one possible response:

Understand where you are.
Er, I'm at home.
Assess where you want to be.
On holiday?
Apply the experience of others to your own situation.
Sue and Pete went to the South of France – perhaps I'll go there.
Identify what you can change.
This skirt?

4

Take action.
Later, I've got to go to work now!

This illustrates two things you'll need if this book is to be any use –
a sense of humour and some imagination. You'll need the first
because, let's face it, books like this can get a bit po-faced and take
themselves far too seriously; and one of the best ways of making
progress in any situation is to see the funny side.

You'll also need imagination because that's central to our whole
approach. Throughout the book we make reference to STEP
activities, and you can find suggestions for specific imaginative
journeys designed to help you assess your situation in our final
chapter. The STEP acronym is widely used for a number of different
ideas – perhaps you'd like to make up your own:

Stand – Tall – Everyone – Please.

Or how about:

Steven and – Tracy's – Enigmatic – Party?

Or,

Some – Tomes – Explain – Patronizingly?

So while we don't claim any great originality for using the word, we
do apply it in a specific way to a range of imaginative exercises:

Step back – review your situation from a more distant perspective.
Take a different view – look at what *you* could change.
Envision – a different future, where things are more in balance.
Prioritize – to begin to make that future a reality.

Use the STEP section of the book in Chapter 5 to help you to
understand where you are and where you want to be – and to begin
to work out how to get there. There's a range of suggested activities:
have a look, maybe have a laugh, and find what's right for you.

At various points in the book we've suggested using STEP
exercises, but see this in the context of a practical book that's
designed to help you make a difference. We suggest that, whenever

there's something that you feel you need to think through, a STEP meditation might be the way forward. If, on the other hand you're the kind of person who doesn't need any of that 'sideways seeing' type of stuff or you get annoyed at having to jump about the book, another way of using the questions we pose is to write down any that seem interesting/relevant to your situation and come back to them later.

Who are we and why are we writing this book?

- Thanks for asking!
- We're married.
- Middle-aged (in years only!).
- Our two teenage children are far more mature than us.
- We write.
- We're not sport fans.
- Gordon has a Dalek on his desk.
- We swim, cycle and one of us goes to the gym for exercise.
- Ronni drives a small purple 'Popemobile'!
- We like to laugh – often at ourselves.
- We both find prayer and meditation important – we each have very different ways of doing them.

How much more do you want? Would you like some measurements? Food, film, plays and books? How about a history of our families? We could go on for ever (and sometimes do), talking about ourselves. We're fascinating, wonderful people but also dreadfully boring if we continue like this!

More seriously, much of the material in this book is based on personal experience. We came to a point where we knew that some things had to change if our family and work were to continue in a symbiotic relationship. This book is not our story, but it does draw on our experience, as well as the experiences of others. We've changed names and disguised details in some instances, or even rolled several experiences into one, but all the case studies in this book are based on real experiences. We'll tell more of our own story, by way of illustration, as the book develops but now it's time to think about you.

You're going to ask yourself some basic questions. By way of illustration here are some questions we consider relevant – and our answers. When you've read what we have to say, look at the questions that follow and have a go yourself.

Q Why are you interested in these issues?

A We both work at busy, demanding jobs that, on the whole we enjoy. We have two children and at times have found it a struggle to balance the needs of the family (including our joy at being part of it), the demands of our jobs, and our need to have time for ourselves.

Q What's good about your jobs?

A Gordon is a producer for BBC Education and enjoys making radio, TV and websites for schools and the general audience. He likes the creativity of his job and has a particular love for radio drama – working with writers and actors and putting the whole thing together in studio.

He likes meeting the audience – especially school users as he can get instant, often critical, feedback.

He also enjoys producing websites, particularly the virtual-community aspects, where he can enable people all over the country (and the world), to dialogue and share ideas.

He values his work colleagues and feels privileged to work with imaginative and creative people.

Ronni is a vicar, working for the Church of England, and she loves it. The job is multi-faceted and she enjoys the people contact best of all.

She's something of a specialist in 'all-age worship' and enjoys helping children to explore their spirituality. She likes to find creative ways to worship, including drama and dance.

The more sombre side of her work involves helping people in difficult times, particularly during and after bereavement. Although 'enjoy' wouldn't be the right word here, she values this side of her vocation [and she's good at it – Gordon]. She also enjoys weddings and baptisms. She's a creative and imaginative 'people person'.

Q What brought things to a head?

A Two factors forced us to reappraise how we live with work. Gordon landed an eight-month 'attachment' within the BBC to look at work–life balance in relation to flexible working. He found himself thinking about the issues and, consequently, changing his working pattern and arrangements. While working on the project, Gordon had no desk at Television Centre – he 'hot desked', making his base at home with a RAS (remote access system) PC to log on to the BBC network and a mobile phone that could pick up emails when he was away from base. He had the opportunity to explore these issues right across the BBC and other organizations, including a meeting with Tony Blair at 10 Downing Street.

Gordon's project involved: seminars across the BBC around the country, where staff were consulted and had their say on the BBC's approach to flexibility; an intranet site for personnel on flexible working and work–life balance; a booklet for staff – *Options for Flexible Working;* a major BBC conference with a contribution from Greg Dyke, chaired by David Aaronovitch; a flexible-working protocol for managers; and establishment of a funded series of pilots – departments and teams trying new and innovative ways of working.

Gordon left the project in June 2000 to return to working in Digital Media and a permanent member of the Human Resources (HR) team took on responsibility for encouraging and supporting flexible working across the BBC.

The other factor was that Ronni had too much to do. Her job (she was then vicar of two churches in Hemel Hempstead) had always been demanding. But as time went on, various factors contrived to make it less and less rewarding. She was working within a complicated local hierarchy, across two very different churches and with a large number of people in her patch. We worked out that once she'd done the basics – preparing and leading Sunday services, preparing and leading weddings, baptisms and funerals, attending to administration and various management meetings – once she'd done all this, she had no time left for the other parts of the job that really make a difference. These would include schools work, visiting, leading devotions, and so on. Of course, she actually did these things, but this was only achievable by working impossible hours. A normal week included six full days and three or four evenings – there was very little time to be a parent, partner, and individual – or just to be. In short, we had a crisis in our work–life balance story in relation to Ronni's job.

Q What changes did you make?

A We really did follow the advice in this book. No really, we're not just making it up as we go along! In fact we did make it up as we went along, but now we're writing it down.

For us, this wasn't a theoretical discussion – it was real. We worked through the issues. We thought, discussed, raged, planned

8

and made changes to our lives because we felt that we had to. If we didn't, something would give; perhaps our health, or our relationship or, our greatest fear, our lifestyles would have an adverse affect on our children. So what did we do?

Lots of things, and many of them impact on what we say throughout the book, but here's a potted history of changes we made to bring some balance back to our lives.

We distributed the chores more evenly. We really did! We now operate a policy of 'whoever gets there first' for the washing, ironing and dishwasher. At the time of writing, the vacuuming is picked up by our son who's desperate to earn extra pocket money for the latest trading card craze (this will be a laughable memory by the time this book is published so we won't mention the name of the cards!). If you find yourself asking about the dusting – simply give us a call and you can do it any time you want.

Ronni put the brakes on. This was the hardest of all the changes we made because it can be very difficult for a vicar to say no. The difficulty was compounded by the number of different circles in which she worked – none of them knew of the work she did for the others, so she was not surprised to hear that in one of her churches some people thought she didn't have enough to do!

Saying no is hard; it causes upset and adds to stress levels. We took this route because we could see no alternative. Looking at the situation intelligently, she had to cut back in order to survive.

Gordon changed his working pattern. As described above, Gordon adopted some flexible working patterns that enabled him to be at home more, or at home at more appropriate times. He switched his thinking from place-based to task-based work, and tried to see his work and the rest of his life more holistically.

We made time for us. During one particularly stressful time we realized that we simply didn't give our relationship the time it needed. We worked hard, with varying success, to put this right and to create more time to do things together. We think it's true to say that we're still working on this, since it's easier to let this slip than to go into battle on other fronts, but we have made progress.

The children grew up. That was a surprise! Almost overnight they were keen to get the house to themselves. Suddenly we didn't have to be with them all the time. It's still changing, of course, as we learn to be parents of adolescents for the first time. This is only slightly better than being an adolescent oneself for the first time.

And in the end. There is no end, because balance is dynamic, shifting, changing. The latest is that Ronni decided to change jobs, feeling that the structure of her post needed to change, and couldn't while she was in place.

This is a big change – one of the most important you can make in readdressing your work–life balance, but sometimes it's the best way forward. It's a bit of a leap in the dark though: will we go from the frying pan to the fire? We don't know, but we do know that, because of the experience of the last few years, we're better equipped to cope.

That's more than enough of us. It's over to you, for some thinking about work–life balance from your perspective. You're doing this for your own interest, and no one else need see it, so you can be more personal and revealing than we have. Use the exercise as a way of exploring what's important to you, what matters in your life as of this moment. Keep your list somewhere safe – unless it's so revealing that you have to destroy it! We'll come back to it later, in Chapter 3.

You might like to start with one of the STEP exercises beginning on page 73. Perhaps use a 'stilling' meditation to let your thoughts settle and allow your creativity to surface. Then use the questions below to help you think about how your work–life balance 'works' at the moment. After the questions, there are some suggestions for how you could assess your responses.

Some initial questions about your work–life balance:

1. When you meet someone for the first time, how do you introduce yourself?
   (a) by your profession or work (as in, 'Hi, I'm an astronaut')
   (b) by your name
   (c) with reference to some other aspect of your life
2. When you think about your work how do you feel?
   (a) excited, positive, lively
   (b) depressed, unhappy, negative
   (c) indifferent
3. Considering the balance between your work and the rest of your life, how do you feel?
   (a) that you spend too much time and energy on your work
   (b) that you spend too little time and energy on your work
   (c) that the balance is about right

4. Which do you consider closer to the 'real you'?
   (a) the person I am at work
   (b) the person I am away from work
   (c) both

5. If you are unable to sleep because of worries and concerns, what are these about?
   (a) mainly work
   (b) mainly things outside work
   (c) both equally, or, I have no worries that keep me awake

6. Do you feel able to make changes to the way you work?
   (a) no
   (b) yes
   (c) don't know

7. What is your main motivation for working?
   (a) money
   (b) fulfilment and human contact
   (c) a balance of (a) and (b)

8. Why are you using this book?
   (a) I have an urgent need to change the way I live with work
   (b) There are some minor aspects I'd like to change
   (c) I feel no need of change, I'm just curious

9. Which of these statements is true for you?
   (a) I find it difficult to stop working
   (b) I know exactly when work stops and 'my' time begins
   (c) a mixture of (a) and (b)

10. After reading and considering these issues, what do you think will happen?
    (a) I am determined to take action to change my work–life balance story
    (b) I might take action to change my work–life balance story
    (c) I will probably not change anything

We hope this exercise has helped you to begin to think through the issues and decide where you are in your own work–life balance story. You can use the above questions simply as 'starters' to set you thinking, or you can use a 'scoring system' to help you codify your responses.

Appraising your results

Balance picture

One way to 'score' your responses is to draw a simple balance (like the one below) at the bottom of a sheet of paper.

Work   Life

/\

Mark one side of the balance as 'Work', and the other as 'Life'. Now look at your responses and add 'weights' to the scale. So if your answer to question 1 makes you think you have your work out of balance with the rest of your life (i.e. work is too pervasive), draw a weight (or weights) on the work side – you can just use crosses or circles if you're not feeling too artistic. Work through the questions adding weights to your picture, until you end up with a graphical representation of how you feel about your work–life balance at the moment.

Statements

Another way of looking at what your answers tell you is to turn them into statements. You might, for example, end up with:

- I find it difficult to stop working.
- I have no worries that keep me awake.
- I have an urgent need to change the way I live with work.

. . . and so on.

When you have a list of statements, place those that seem most important to you at the top, to create a prioritized list of comments about work–life balance. What does the order of the statements tell you? Can you sum up the message of your answers in one simple clear assessment – it might be something like, 'Normally, I have a good work–life balance, but at the moment work is taking over my life and I have to do something about it.'

Or it could be, 'I've discovered how little time I give to important relationships – something has to give and I'll work smarter to make more time.'

12

Interview yourself

Using your answers to the questions, write an interview with yourself about your approach to work–life issues at the moment. You could use our 'interview' on page 10 as a guide, asking yourself questions such as:

- Why are you interested in these issues at the moment?
- How healthy do you feel your work–life balance is at present?
- What are the main difficulties you're experiencing as you try to get your work–life balance right?
- What do you like about your work?
- What would you like to make more time for?
- Do you have any ideas for specific changes you could make?
- Do you have a clear picture of where you want to be?

Mini case studies

Now that you've begun to think about your work–life balance, you might be feeling excited at the possibilities, or depressed at the impossibilities! Below are some tasters of the way that people have changed their work–life balance stories. They're all based on real cases and we hope they illustrate what's possible in a variety of circumstances.

Holiday job

Sue works for a large organization. A few years ago she began to find it difficult to balance her childcare responsibilities with the demands of her job. She worked out that if she rearranged her workload she could take additional leave each year to allow her not to work during the school holidays. Her manager supported the plan and Sue's salary was spread equally over the year so that she didn't have to survive the long summer holiday with no pay.

Shhh!

Derek, an executive with a large multinational was getting into the office at 7.00 each day in order to do two hours' work before most people arrived. He found that a lot of his colleagues were doing the same! Then he heard about 'quiet time' – a simple idea that involved everyone agreeing that from 9.00 to 11.00 each morning, only

13

essential emails, calls and discussions would take place. The focus during those hours was on a quiet, peaceful start to the day when everyone could concentrate on their own work. Derek and his colleagues discovered that they no longer needed to come to the office so early, and just as much work was done.

Closed-door policy

Samina worked in an open-plan office, processing expense claims. She liked the opportunity to be around her colleagues and she supported the company's open-plan ethos. She noted, however, that her boss had an office and that her boss could shut the office door when she wanted some peace and quiet. Samina bought a small flag and some Blu-Tack to stand it in. She explained to her colleagues that when the flag was up, her door was shut and she shouldn't be disturbed. She found that a couple of hours a day of 'flag up time' made a huge difference to her work. Soon the whole office was competing with their own versions of the flag – one person put on a hat, another had a toy alligator whose appearance on her computer meant, 'Keep away, I bite when disturbed!'

The flexible team

Alice, a manager of a small sales team, was getting lots of requests for flexible and part-time working and was having difficulty accommodating and keeping track of her team. She bought the team together one morning and laid out the issues before them, explaining the company's needs as well as supporting the desire for flexibility in the team. The she handed it over to them, asking the team to come up with a workable solution that would give everyone something of what they wanted and still allow the sales office to function effectively.

A week later they submitted their proposals, and within a month the new arrangements were being piloted. The team adjusted the working patterns as they went along and now completely manage their own flexibility.

Driven

Adrian found the long drive to and from work frustrating; he would often finish work by 7 p.m., but not be home until after 9 p.m. when his young children were in bed. There was a good deal of stress in the home, because of the long-hours culture at Adrian's workplace, and this was not helped when his manager flatly refused to consider Adrian's plan to work at home two days a week.

He decided to leave his job and take a less stressful one, nearer to home, at a lower salary. He adjusted his ambitions, seeing that at this period in his life he needed to give more time to his family. On balance he feels that the change has been beneficial and he has hopes of getting a better paid, but more flexible, job soon.

Changes to the way people can work are explored more fully in the next chapter, but we hope these glimpses have inspired you to think that it is possible – in small or large ways – to change the way you live with work.

Here's one last mini case study to end this chapter. Gordon and Ronni found that there was always so much to do when working at home that they didn't take proper breaks. Their daughter kept pushing them to get a dog and eventually the harassed parents gave in. Guess what? As soon as they acquired their eccentric Labrador, they had to take regular breaks. They didn't just talk about work–life balance, they lived it:

Talk the talk
Walk the talk
Walk the dog!

You know it makes sense.

Key issues

- Balance is dynamic – keep thinking creatively about changing and adapting.
- Understand where you are now and where you want to be.
- Take action – practical steps such as sharing chores and being prepared to say no.
- Learn from the experience of others.
- Exercises to help you assess where you are in your work–life balance story.

2
Work in balance

There are a number of reasons why the balance between work and the rest of life is suddenly high on the agendas of many companies and organizations around the world. In brief, there are six key factors that have all come together to stimulate change:

- Societal changes including increased caring responsibilities and two partners working.
- Traffic and travel overcrowding including environmental costs and parking congestion.
- New communications technologies make it possible to work in ways undreamed of just a few years ago.
- The move to a 24-hour global culture that requires flexible working practices.
- Pressure to reduce expensive office space.
- Lifestyle changes – including some younger people not willing to buy into the all-hours culture of the past.

We'll be looking at these in more detail and asking how they affect you later in the chapter, but first look at these statements and see if you agree with any of them:

The world of work has changed a lot since I was a child.
People think about work differently these days.
I can think of several acquaintances who work outside the traditional working hours/place culture.
I can think of several ways that technology has changed working life in the last few years.
Traffic and travel congestion make working lives more difficult.
Caring responsibilities for young and old are more complex these days.
I am aware of working hours changing and the move to a 24-hour, 7-days-a-week culture.
I want more time for other (non-work) things in my life.
At work a lot of money is wasted on empty desks and unused equipment.
People are generally more productive than they used to be.
People are generally less productive than they used to be.

Looking at your responses to the above statements, which of the following best sums up your place in the world of work at the moment?

- I'm in the middle of a lot of change – I'm finding it confusing and uncomfortable.
- Things seem pretty much as they always were for me but I can see change elsewhere.
- We're in a time of gradual, evolutionary change and development.
- Things are changing – and about time too.

Whatever your own personal response, you'll see that this is all about change. That dynamic balance that we met in the first chapter is rearing its head again. We are constantly living with change in all areas of our lives. Change can overwhelm you, you can ride it like a wave, or you can influence it. For most of us, most of the time, our attitudes and response to change are a mixture of all three; but we'd like to manage change better by knowing what we can influence, what we can ignore and when we have to accept change and ride with it. The first step in this process is understanding, so we'll move on now to look in a little more detail at those drivers for change in the work–life balance story.

A note to employers

This book is primarily addressed to those in work rather than employers, and we're aware that we're asking for a lot of flexibility and challenging some well established and comfortable ways of doing things. Throughout the book we encourage employees to look critically and to ask for change. Employers might feel they're expected to give and give and give again. Some may feel that their profits are under threat or that they are being asked to act as a sponge for social pressures and problems. Our view on this is that the key message to organizations about societal change is that it's *here now*, it continues to evolve and it is real. In other words:

Adapting your organization to fit the needs of your staff is not optional. Organizations that do not recognize this reality, that do not change, will suffer in the new world of work.

Or to put it another way:

This is not primarily about the social case or being a good employer. It is about adapting to labour market conditions. If you want the best people, listen to how they want to work and bend over backwards to accommodate them. If you don't do this, your competitors will.

Having said that, and said it somewhat forcefully, we recognize that each situation is different and not all the ideas will be practical for every circumstance. The best way forward has to be what we call a 'partnership of outcomes', that is:

- Look at what the organization wants to achieve and how.
- Look at what the individual wants to achieve and how.
- See where these can fruitfully converge.
- Agree together where there are areas of give and take.
- Try it out and keep flexible!

Societal changes

When Gordon attended the launch of Employers for Work–Life Balance at Downing Street on behalf of the BBC, the Prime Minister gave a prepared speech about the importance of the initiative. Everyone listened in respectful silence as their breakfasts grew cold, but there was an extra attentiveness as Tony Blair put down the prepared notes and spoke of the changes he'd seen in the world of work. He spoke about his parents, about his mother being devoted to her work of bringing up the children and holding the family together while her husband played the traditional role, for those times, of breadwinner. The Prime Minister said what a debt he owed to his mother, and how important her role was. Then he contrasted this with today. He's part of a very modern family structure with both husband and wife in demanding jobs. He made the point that employers can't afford to wish things were different, the clock couldn't be turned back, and he wouldn't want to. Change in family structures had occurred and was occurring. Employers, living in the real world, had to cope with this change and see it as an advantage, not a problem.

We shouldn't get too carried away with the Blair household as an example. They have many advantages that the rest of us would like plenty of money, for example. They also have severe disadvantages – lack of privacy and press interest in their every move. But the Prime Minister's point is true for all of us. There has been a revolution in the world of work over the past 50 years and this has been driven by, and has driven societal change:

- There are many more working women than when Tony was a child.
- Families and individuals are far more mobile.
- There are more single parent families.
- There is a richer blend of cultural traditions.
- People change jobs more often.
- Consumerism, the explosion of leisure activities and the service sector have revolutionized the kind of work many people do.
- As people live longer, so eldercare becomes a bigger factor in many lives, with people caring for children and older relatives at the same time.

All of these factors have influenced when, where, and how work is done. Perhaps the biggest of these drivers for change, in relation to work–life balance has been the rise in numbers and in status of women in paid work. There is still some way to go until equality is achieved in terms of pay and status, but we are in the midst of big change. An enormous amount of talent, experience and skill has become available in the workplace. The more demanding side of this is that parents have had to become more imaginative with their childcare. We touch on this in Chapter 4, but the important point here is that employers now have to be more imaginative and creative too. Society needs parents to parent, but we are beginning to realize how, with flexibility on all sides, this important role can be combined with work. Here are a few examples of different approaches to combining work and childcare:

Parent Managing Director

Jenny and Peter run their own media business. They set it up specifically so that they could share their work and their childcare responsibilities. Each was working full-time in different companies but they felt that they didn't want to miss out on their young son's early years. They're now joint MDs of their own company, and work three days each in the office – they're together at work for half a day for a handover. They each get lots of time with their son, and time for themselves and they're building a business together.

Flexi-child

Patricia and Lindsay are life partners who both work and have a young child. Lindsay's job takes her away from home about one week in six. Patricia tries to book in working at home as much as possible during these times. They make up the rest of their childcare with a regular, but flexible arrangement with a childminder.

Mother and daughter and daughter

Alex is a single parent. She has moved to live near her mum, who takes some of the childcare responsibility for Alex's daughter Holly. Another reason for the move was to get a job with a workplace nursery. Holly is on the waiting list and when a place becomes available for her Alex will move from part-time to full-time work.

In these three examples we see different approaches – the world of work adapting to societal change. Jenny and Peter have taken the self-help route to its extreme, by starting their own company. You may not be able to go this far, but their flexible arrangement typifies a twenty-first-century approach to work that looks at life holistically and attempts to combine the different elements into a satisfying and viable lifestyle.

Patricia and Lindsay have adapted their lifestyle to their circumstances. There is a telling give and take about their approach and a pragmatic attempt to put the different parts of their lives together.

Alex has a workable partnership with her mother, but also with her employer who recognizes the value she brings to the organization and is prepared to be flexible by offering her part-time work for now, and a place for Holly at a subsidized nursery.

All three examples represent the kind of flexibility that is needed in the new world of work if employers are to get the best out of their people. Imagine, for example, how much less productive Alex would be if she were constantly worrying about Holly. This flexible approach also means that employees are happier in their work, which must make them better at it. Notice, however, that in the examples we've picked, it's the individuals, not the organizations, who've been most creative and flexible. This is changing, but the rate of change needs to speed up and more employers need to recognize that:

- People are an organization's most valuable asset.
- The world of work is changing to a 24-hour/7-days-a-week culture – organizations need flexibility.
- Staff have many conflicting pressures on them – they need flexibility.
- A workforce that feels valued will produce work of value.

This last point is really the key message for successful organizations in the new century of work. The process is cyclic.

Staff feel valued

⤴   ⤵

Organization recognizes   Staff are better motivated
that success is built
on people

⤶   ⤴

Organization is
more successful

Traffic and travel

Samina and Josh live close to Josh's workplace in Hemel Hempstead. He can walk to the office if he chooses (about 40 minutes), bike it if he's feeling fit, catch a bus, take the car, get a lift . . . About the only thing he can't do to get to work is fly – yet.

Samina works in publishing in West London. To travel by public transport she has two options.

Option one:

Walk, bike, drive, or get a lift to the bus depot.
Get a bus to Central London, then a Tube to near her place of work.

Option two:

Walk, bike, drive, or get a lift to the railway station.
Then a train and two Tubes.

She finds that either public transport option is unpredictable with too many opportunities for things to go wrong. She used the train and Tube method for five years, but found she was arriving at work tense – particularly if she had to hit a particular time for a meeting. On many occasions one or more of the services would break down or run late. She had to massively overestimate travel times and still often arrived late for meetings.

She now drives. Her journey takes between one and two hours each way, depending on the time of travel. There is limited car parking space at her office and Samina has to beg, borrow or steal car parking tickets from a pool held in her department.

However she chooses to do it, getting to work is often more stressful than actually doing any work. The time spent travelling is wasted. She can't work in the car and the trains are too crowded. For Samina and thousands like her there has to be a better way.

Samina's boss, Gary, is concerned about Samina. He feels she's not at her creative best at the moment and he's right. She's drained, tired and resentful of the pressure that travel to work is adding to her life. Gary values Samina and wants to get more out of her. He wants her to be happy at work because, as a thoughtful manager, he knows that this will be good for the organization. For Gary, and thousands like him, there has to be a better way.

Samina often drives in at peak time. She joins thousands of cars on the M1 and the crowded roads around West London. Many of the cars carry only one person. She knows she's adding to pollution, she knows she's adding to environmental blight for the people who live around her route; and she knows that roads are expensive to make and repair. Samina is very aware that, by getting to work this way, she is part of a circle of distress for her country's infrastructure. For this country, and countries all over the world, there has to be a better way.

A better way?

Just give your heart to the god of balance and everything will be fine! So we sound like evangelists preaching to you about your sins before cajoling you into signing up for our miracle cure. We're not really suggesting a miraculous change, but there are very simple and pragmatic ways of adapting how we work. A small act of will and we could move a long way to undoing the damage that Samina's journey to work does to her, her organization and the country. Samina has several options, as described below.

Time travel

Samina could change the times at which she travels to and from work so that she avoids rush-hour traffic. The effects of this would be a small reduction in pollution because her car's engine wouldn't be running for so long. There'd be a big reduction in her stress levels because her journeys would be smoother. She'd not be contributing to those traffic peaks that make life so unpleasant for local residents – but she would be contributing to traffic throughout the day in those areas, which might not be helpful.

Her manager, Gary, would have to buy into this new arrangement and see that the advantages of a less stressed Samina would outweigh the difficulties in reorganizing meeting times and being flexible about when Samina was physically in the office. Gary may find that reorganizing his use of time has other benefits: starting meetings later gives people time to prepare and allows a 'quiet time' for focused individual work at the start of the day.

This option has some advantages for Samina, but it doesn't offer much help on the pollution or local congestion fronts.

Stay at home

Samina could spend some time each week working at home. She would be able to focus on tasks for which the busy and sometimes noisy office is a disadvantage:

- There is no travel pollution.
- There is no residential congestion.
- She can keep in touch through phone, PC, Internet, fax, etc.
- She suffers no travel stress.

The above advantages, however, are based on certain assumptions:

- Samina's work can accommodate this approach.
- She has somewhere quiet to work at home.
- Her organization can equip her with the necessary technology.

Gary would need to buy in completely to make this work, but in publishing many of Samina's tasks could be done this way with a probable increase in efficiency. In order to manage this properly, Gary and Samina would need to agree and regularly review some ground rules on how often Samina would need to come to the office; which parts of her work required face-to-face contact; and so on.

Super flex

This is the most radical, yet in some ways the most practical option. Gary needs to recognize that in order to get the best out of Samina, and to keep her with the organization as long as possible, he should try to tailor her working environments and times to best suit her way of working and her lifestyle needs.

The process starts with a step back, looking at all the aspects of Samina's work and breaking them down into tasks. Gary and Samina might end up with a list like this:

Regular tasks
Managing projects
Managing staff
Reviewing budgets
Pitching ideas
Mentoring junior colleagues
Editing texts

Occasional tasks
Interviewing staff
Sitting on review boards
Organizing office socials

Fuzzy-edged tasks
Being around
Picking up and contributing to organizational culture
Being part of creative buzz

The next step is to look at where each task is best carried out, taking into account the waste of time spent travelling and the other factors listed above. The list might then look something like this:

Regular tasks	
Managing projects	Home
Managing staff	Home/Office

Reviewing budgets	Home
Pitching ideas	Office
Mentoring junior colleagues	Office
Editing texts	Home

Occasional tasks

Interviewing staff	Office
Sitting on review boards	Office
Organizing office socials	Home/Office

Fuzzy-edged tasks

Being around	Office
Picking up and contributing to organizational culture	Office
Being part of creative buzz	Office

It looks from the above as though Samina could spend about a third of her time at home if things could be properly organized for her. So far this solution is pretty much like 'Stay at home' above, but here's where it could get interesting. Supposing Samina and Gary revolutionized the way that they thought about work. Having identified that things can happen in different places, what if they forgot about the places for a moment and thought instead about the tasks? What if they moved to a completely task-focused way of thinking about work? This might have the following outcomes:

- Samina would agree her tasks with Gary.
- He would then leave her to get on with them.
- She would go where she needed to undertake each task – office, home, a cottage in Wales, her sister's . . .
- She would work when it was most appropriate. It might suit her to work a couple of evenings and take time off on Friday, for example.
- Her work and home life would be in much better balance.
- She'd waste less time travelling.
- The environment would benefit.
- The organization would benefit.

In the above response to travel congestion, we've mostly thought about office-based or home-based working, but there is a new alternative emerging. What if three people working on a project simply find a space close to where they live – or midway between the three of them? This might involve less travel for all of them with the consequent advantages for them and the environment. They could hire a room, or meet in a pub or motorway services. With the latest technology, this can be just like meeting in the office and may move more of those 'office-based' tasks away from base.

It can happen and it can work in such a way that everyone's a winner – you just have to believe, don't you? Actually, this kind of approach takes much more than faith and commitment because to really work it needs a radical change in the culture of an organization. Perhaps you've been reading the above and thinking:

Sure – lovely theory, but I know it wouldn't work for my job; and even if it could work for me, it would just throw bigger burdens on everyone left behind. One person's flexible lifestyle is another person's increase in stress as they pick up the pieces.

Or, to take another 'realistic' angle, Gordon recently spoke at a conference where a manager said something like:

My part of the organization is committed to flexible working and we have many examples to demonstrate this. But I have to say as a manager that I'm finding it increasingly difficult to schedule my people – with part-time workers needing to fit alongside home workers, and so on. There are deadlines to meet and, although we've bent over backwards to accommodate people, there comes a point where you have to say no to some requests.

We're talking in this section about the travel pressures that face individuals and organizations, but this is only one factor among those listed at the top of this chapter that are forcing organizations to rethink their culture in relation to when and how work is done. Our answer to the real objections raised by staff and managers starts by recognizing that the world of work has changed and is continuing to change. The travel problems are real, as are the societal changes we wrote about earlier; as are the communication changes, cost reduction options, the global culture and lifestyle changes that we'll consider next. For managers and workers alike, the starting point can no longer be the needs of the organization alone. Any company that fails to take note of all these changes will simply lose its best people to other, more flexible organizations. Or they will keep them – but keep them unhappy, unfulfilled and unable to work at their best. To the manager who doesn't know if she can continue to say yes to requests for flexibility, our message is – it's worse than you think! You need to move your thinking from a mid-twentieth-century to a twenty-first-century view of work. Work now is about a partnership, one that takes into account the whole person. Your staff offer you a part of their time, their creativity, their lives – and nothing is more precious. They will negotiate with you which part and how they will manage the agreed tasks. You'll offer a reward, mostly monetary, for this arrangement. So it's no longer a question of what you will let them do, it's a negotiation in which they will want to balance work with the rest of their lives and the manager will want to balance the tasks that need doing. Twenty-first-century managers recognize this fundamental shift and embrace it because they know they will get the very best out of their workforce by seeing work in its proper perspective.

New technologies

Andrew's alarm woke him at the usual time and prepared his breakfast, gave him the day's news and reminded him of the deadlines and tasks of the day ahead. After eating and the morning ablutions Andrew decided to do some work. Would it be Coventry, London or Atlanta first today? The last of these would still be asleep of course so he'd start there – ease himself into the day.

He put on his headset, selected the Atlanta office and was soon engaged in a meeting with the American team. They'd all been at the meeting yesterday but had edited the important bits for him and asked for his views on some crucial details of the proposed leisure development. Wandering around the boardroom during the meeting, Andrew took a good look at the latest model and made his mind up. He'd never been happy with the landscaping and now he asked the room to set up a meeting later in the day when he could put his objections to the team. His business done, he walked through the door into Coventry . . .

Our apologies if you feel as though you've just walked into the wrong book. In the above example, Andrew's working environment is almost entirely virtual, so he can freely and effectively move across the world and look at detailed recordings of previous events – all from the confines of his home. Technology isn't quite that advanced yet, but you could perform any of the tasks that Andrew did in our piece of future gazing, today – now. You could view a video of yesterday's meeting – send your own views by PC camera or email, and look at a 3D computer-generated model all at the same time. You could look at the model in conversation with people all over the world and you could watch them as they point to features or sketch ideas in real time.

The solution to many of the problems posed by the changing world of work lies in technology. How relevant this is to you will depend on the nature of your job and your personal style and circumstances, but one way forward is to assess your work tasks using a table like the one opposite.

Filling in a table like this will help you to explore the possibilities of technology for changing where, when and how we work. But . . .

Beware the dark side!

Technology is out of control – like Dr Frankenstein we have created a monster that has turned upon us, crushing . . . Sorry, we got a bit carried away again! But there is a less positive side to technology because when you allow communications equipment to create a bridge between your home and work, you are extending the workplace into your home. This is great when it works for you – allowing you to sleep in, avoid the traffic, take the children to school and still respond to 50 emails before your boss has entered the car park. It's less than great when it allows your boss to call you just as you're settling down to a quiet evening with your partner, with the news that she's emailed you a report and she'd like a response by 9 a.m. tomorrow. In the days before all this wonderful comm. – tech stuff, the report would have had to wait until tomorrow morning. Progress cuts both ways.

This is a situation that we've long lived with, being a vicarage family with Ronni's work based in the family home. Here are our tips for turning the link to work into a swing bridge, with your hands on the controls:

- Get an answerphone and put it on when you want to get some time to yourself – meal times, days off, etc.
- Get an extra phone line (your work might pay for it). Only give out your private number to your friends and family, don't let work colleagues get hold of it. You can then put on the answer phone on the work line or just ignore it when you're not working.

WORK IN BALANCE

Task	Technology used at base	Could task be done elsewhere?	Technology needed to move task

- Develop a polite way of telling callers when you're working and when you're not.
- If practical, let work colleagues know in advance when you're going to be working. An email saying you're at home on Friday but finishing work early – so please call before 4.00 – should do the trick.
- Get separate email accounts for work and home – simple and free these days.

The move to a 24-hour global culture requires flexible working

No doubt about it, the old pattern of five days of 9–5 followed by two days off is breaking down. Of course, for many people such as shift workers, doctors and armed service personnel, to name a few, it never existed anyway. More and more of us will find that we are working a flexible pattern of days and hours. Is this good news or bad? Neither – it's just news – to many of you it probably isn't even that.

Let's imagine that your organization is asking you to work in a new pattern. The key question is whether this will work to your advantage. We'll start by taking an overview, looking at some of the factors operating here:

- You're important to the organization so your needs matter to them.
- If your lifestyle is completely incompatible with what they have on offer you'll look for a more up-to-date approach elsewhere.
- If you do have to compromise and work some hours that don't suit, you should expect to be well compensated either with money, extra time off or both.
- You might need to adjust your lifestyle to fit, but this could have benefits (if you can cope with it, doing the shopping in a 24-hour supermarket at 3 a.m. could have advantages).

Our advice can only be general but for what it's worth; if you're faced with working odd patterns that don't seem to suit your lifestyle, consider the following:

- *Think different.* Don't just react that it doesn't suit, it could be that *you're* living in the past and not adapting to the new world of work. Look at any positive benefits the new pattern could offer before being critical.
- *Think balance.* Weigh up the negatives and positives to help you decide if it's worth persevering by attempting to deal with things you don't like.
- *Think creative.* What are the stumbling-blocks – childcare, time for relationships, problems finding time for your hobby? Take a creative look at the situation; are there different ways of organizing these aspects of your life that would enable you to fit the new work pattern?
- *Think assertive.* Having looked across the piece and examined it from all angles, are there things you'd like to put to the organization? Can you suggest some modifications to the working pattern that would make it better for you, or can you argue that the cost of the disruption requires a higher reward – perhaps more time off during the school holidays, for example?

Change, or the threat of it, can be enormously upsetting and, if you are faced with this sort of disruption, the best thing you can do is to gain a sense of perspective. Use a STEP exercise (see page 74), to help you think through the issues and find your route to a solution.

Pressure on expensive office space

This is one of the big drivers for changing when and where people work. The cost of office space and other overheads can add 40 per cent to the cost of employing someone, so it's no wonder that companies and organizations try to cut costs by using the space more productively or by having people work at home.

Many modern offices would resemble battery farms if you were able to fly over the heads of the busy workers as they sit in their low-walled cubicles each with its carefully measured designated space, its identical desk, chair and PC. This arrangement seems to be inviting people to say 'Let me out, I want to work somewhere nicer, more stimulating, more fitted to being human.' We all know that the bottom line is the bottom line, that organizations have to maximize profits, give the very best value for money – and the battery farm office is one way of doing this. But as with everything in the work–life balance story, there's a dynamic tension here also. If your organization needs to get anything out of you that is creative, inspired, visionary, fun or uses your brainpower to the full, then the organization should provide an environment that stimulates these qualities. Here are some cost-effective – keep the bottom line happy – solutions to that pressure on expensive desk space:

• Recognize that different tasks need different environments.
• Recognize that individuals each have their own way of working and try to create a flexible space that will have something to suit everyone's style.
• Turn some office cubicles into hot desks and maximize their use. Use the money saved to create some more relaxed and inspiring spaces.
• Allow people to work at home when the task suits – see above – this will also be good for the bottom line, releasing pressure on that expensive office space.
• Involve the teams that will use the space in its design.

The office space issue is a good example of how what's good for the organization is also good for the individual. Once you stop seeing it as a problem it can release all sorts of creative possibilities for changing the world of work to everyone's advantage.

Lifestyle changes

This book and the events, thinking and experience that lead up to it, are symptomatic of the fact that people are thinking differently about work. They are redefining what work is, when it happens, how and where it occurs:

• Many young people don't wish to follow their parents' example. They want to work and be committed to a job, but they want to keep this in perspective and not allow it to take over their lives. They have a more holistic approach to work.
• A number of older people, already established in work, have downsized, taken less stressful jobs and taken a pay cut in order to

allow them time for other things such as hobbies, interests and families.

- Some people have recognized that they have a number of talents, skills and interests that cannot be fed by one job, so they have developed a portmanteau lifestyle in which they combine a number of paid, unpaid and voluntary interests.
- A common route out of traditional single-employer work has been through consultancy – an option often taken up by those taking early retirement. This gives the individual much greater control over his or her own destiny, allowing individuals to pick and choose jobs and how much they work.

Each of the above represents fresh thinking about work for most people, and these new ways of looking at employment chime happily with the theme of this book – the need to see work as a part of who you are, and to create a balance between work and the rest of your life.

When Ronni first started being a vicar we were completely knocked for six by the change in our lifestyle. Her hours were varied, often involving very full days and evenings, and we found we were struggling to cope with the effects on our relationship and family. It took us a while to realize that the biggest mistake we'd made was in defining ourselves too much by our jobs. We had to see that, for each of us, there was a 'me' beneath the roles of vicar, mother, father, lover, producer . . . Work is so important and so all, enveloping in our lives but it is not our lives, it is not 'us'. If you find that your work is taking over your sense of you – either by long or difficult working hours, or by not being able to switch off – it's time to gain some perspective and that's what we look at in the next chapter.

Key issues

- The world of work is changing rapidly due to:
  - changes in society
  - transport issues
  - new communication technologies
  - the emergence of a 24/7 culture
  - cost of space.

- Message to employers – consider the 'partnership of outcomes'.
- View your work and life holistically.
- Lifestyle changes and challenges.
- Analyse your current workload and priorities.
- Cyclic nature of a healthy work–life balance – what's good for you can be good for the organization.
- With imagination and commitment there are always other options.

3

You and work in balance

In this chapter we're going to look at some of the practical steps you can take to change how work and the rest of your life is integrated. Many of the initiatives and changes we've explored so far in this book operate on a large scale with a societal or even global impact. We've looked at new working patterns, travel issues and changes in caring responsibilities. All of these are important factors and they have already, or soon will, impact on how we all work; but what about *you, now*? Are there things that you can do to short-circuit all this, so that you don't have to hang about waiting for the wheels of change to slowly make a difference in your situation?

It will come as no surprise that we believe there are such things and, as ever with this book, the trick is to take our suggestions and the experience of others and apply them to your own situation. As mentioned in Chapter 1, for change to be effective, you need to know where you're heading. You might find it helpful to do one of the STEP exercises beginning on page 73. Ask yourself the following questions:

- What one aspect of my work–life balance would I most like to change?
- What are the obstacles stopping me from making the change?
- What do I need to do to begin to move those blocks?
- What is stopping me from starting?
- How can I take the first step in changing this situation?

Let's take a look at some answers to these questions. Graham works in new media, producing websites. Here are his responses to the above:

Q What one aspect of my work–life balance would I most like to change?
A I'd like to work at home two days a week so that I can share in the childcare to a greater extent.
Q What are the obstacles stopping me from making the change?
A My boss has recently announced that, although she's sympathetic to flexible working issues, she needs to build a stronger team focus and she wants all producers to be around the office as much as possible.

Q What do I need to do to begin to move those obstacles?
A I need to understand that my boss has a good point but that I also have important needs. I should talk frankly and openly with my boss.
Q What is stopping me from starting?
A I'm nervous about her reaction – concerned that she'll think I'm not committed or that I haven't listened to her position on this issue.
Q How can I take the first step in changing this situation?
A Think through the issue; be sure of what I want to say, then go to see my boss at the earliest opportunity. I know I'm a valued member of staff and she's reasonable most of the time. After all, I'm only asking.

Graham did see his boss about this issue and took some ideas with him about flexi-time, email access from home and some specific projects that would be suited to home working. He also pointed out that, if he comes into the office every day, on an average week he spends 15 hours in the car – nearly two days of no use to him, his organization or his family. This last point persuaded his manager to let him try working at home more for a trial period.

We're jumping a little ahead of ourselves here since we've gone straight from stepping back, through formulating plans, to taking action and getting a result! But it is important to see how, in this real-life example, actual change can be initiated through taking time to think things through.

Some other questions you might want to think about as you reflect on your current situation are:

- Where do I currently waste time and energy – can this be avoided or minimized for the benefit of work or other areas of my life?
- Am I employing my talents, skills and experience in the best way for my work and other areas of my life?
- Am I spending too much time worrying about what other people will think?
- What's really good about my working life at the moment – what would I hate to lose?
- What's really good about other areas of my life at the moment – what would I hate to lose?

When you've spent some time thinking through these issues – the here and now of your work and lifestyle balance, it's a good idea to write down some aims for change. You might find it helpful to use a

Things I want to change			
Top priority	Obstacles to change	First step	Record progress
Other priorities			

table like this. Then set aside some time to look at your progress week by week.

From here on, it's very much up to you to apply the most appropriate developments to your own situation. The suggestions below are based on what we and others have discovered. Take these ideas and see what relevance they have (or you can *make* them have) to your own situation.

Changing how and when you work

Start by asking yourself some hard and searching questions about how and when you work. Look for an extreme example to get your creative juices flowing. Is there an aspect of your work that you do because it's always been done that way? Perhaps there's a part of your job that's clearly a bit daft but no one's ever bothered to challenge it? Maybe there's simple reorganization that's obvious to you but you've never had the courage to suggest it.

Examples of each of the above would be:

- Meetings that happen on a regular basis, take a long time and where very little gets done. Ask yourself what is the purpose of such meetings. Do they have a purpose? Are there clearly defined aims and are outcomes expected? If not, what's the point? People often say that the real point of such meetings is the social cohesion of the team. Fine, make that the stated aim and then ask if the meetings are really achieving it! It may be that there are better ways of fulfilling this objective.
- Filling in complicated paperwork or computerized forms. Ask someone what happens to these when they reach the end of the chain. Is all the information used? Does it achieve anything or does it just clog up file or disk space?
- Take a look at *where* things happen. Is anyone, possibly you, travelling on a regular basis to a meeting? Could the meeting be elsewhere? Could it be a virtual meeting – perhaps for three weeks out of four with the fourth meeting a face-to-face event? One group of workers moved their regular team meeting to a variety of pubs and cafés – each chosen to be near the home of a team member. This gave each person in turn a chance for a late start and the informal settings added a welcome relaxed quality to the meetings.

What are your examples of unhelpful ways of doing things? Look back at your list of things you'd like to change. Can you re-categorize them? Use the table opposite to help you.

Having identified some changes you'd like to make, the next step is to formulate an action plan to help you effect real change. As ever, only you will know your own situation and the personalities involved, but here are some general principles and pointers that should help:

- Consider the issue in the round, not just your own situation but also the wider context. Can you demonstrate how this change will benefit you, your colleagues, the organization and your clients/customers/audience? Can you throw in some beneficial effects for society at large and the environment?
- Formulate a plan that will enable you and others to assess the effects of your proposed change. Set targets and assessment

I'd like to change the timing of . . .

I'd like to change the location of . . .

I'd like to change the way we . . .

points. It will be in your interest to acquire evidence of how well (or otherwise) your scheme is working.

- Be prepared to be flexible and adapt to circumstances – the best plans change as they are worked out in practice. Often the best time to finalize goals and outcomes is not at the beginning of a project or change of working practice, but after the scheme is under way and you've begun to see how it works out.

- Take account of personalities, particularly in relation to learning and working styles. The benefits of your plan may be obvious to you, but does everyone else see it that way? Some people might not want to go home earlier – the office might be their sanctuary from an uncreative or oppressive home. They might have their best friends at work and feel most 'at home' there. Also consider the fact that people have different rates of responding to change and varying degrees of success when confronted by new ways of working.

- Work with others. If at all possible, get others on your side before you present your ideas. Get as wide an input as you can. This will make your ideas stronger and more rounded. It will also mean that you've thought through many of the objections you might meet. Your management team are more likely to listen to a group of you than one individual.

- Be sensitive to the psychology of the situation when you talk to your manager(s) – take too many people along and the manager(s) might feel pressured and respond negatively. Choose your moment and consider the best way to play it. Human nature suggests that you'll need to indicate clearly what's in it for the manager(s) – improved morale, for example. And if you can arrange to let some of the glory for these innovative new arrangements shine on the manager(s) . . .

It may be that you are generally happy about the when and how of work, but you'd like to suggest some changes to integrate better the different aspects of your life. Here are some suggestions.

Childcare facilities

Does your employer offer any help for childcare? It could be a workplace nursery or a block booking of places at a local facility. It could even be a scheme such as extra leave for parents on the first day of the school term. Find out what's available, and if you have

40

suggestions why not get together with other like-minded people to put a proposal to management? See next tip!

Parents' group

Many organizations have a working parents' forum where issues about integrating family life and work can be aired and explored. Such a group can be supportive both in giving the opportunity to talk things through and in formulating action plans. Meeting at lunchtime to share sandwiches and chat can be a first step towards structural and cultural change that can benefit the individual, his or her family and the organization. If you don't have such a group at your workplace, this might be the time and you might be the person to set one up.

What's on offer?

If your organization has a personnel or HR department, ask them about their policies related to flexible working and work–life balance. This whole area has an enhanced profile at the start of the new century, and many employers have recognized the sound business case for offering flexibility and tailoring working arrangements to individual need as far as possible. Employers and employees can get advice and support from organizations such as:

- Employers for Work–Life Balance
- The National Work Life Forum
- Parents at Work
- Family Friendly
- The Department for Education and Skills
- Trade unions and professional bodies.

Self-organizing teams

Many managers find the multiplicity of requests for flexible working confusing and even intimidating. Life was so much simpler when everyone worked the same hours! Now the poor manager can't keep track of who's coming in late, who's working at home, who's on one-week-on-one-week-off, and so on.

One solution is to hand the whole thing over to the team. The manager in effect is saying, 'Okay, you want all these different arrangements, the organization needs the team to meet these objectives, you get together and work out how to do it.'

The great advantages of this approach are:

41

- Everyone is involved
- It encourages team members to take responsibility for their working lives.
- It requires a rounded view that takes account of individual, team and organizational needs.
- A complex task is shared.

Teams that adopt this way of working feel more involved with, and more trusted by their organization, and meeting objectives becomes more personalized. The team as a whole and as individuals become stakeholders in the success of the enterprise, and are motivated to prove the business case for giving individuals flexibility.

Take your holidays

If you're looking at the above heading and thinking, *What are they talking about? It's just too obvious*, then you can probably skip this bit. But believe it or not, there are people who simply do not take all the holiday they're entitled to. We are not those people. We plan our holidays, our staying with friends or short breaks away at the start of the year and book them in – we make work fit around them. Perhaps this is because we live in a vicarage with the implication that if you're there, you're available (if someone comes to the door desperately seeking the vicar because they're upset or tragedy has struck, you can't really say, 'Sorry, she's on holiday at home having a nice relaxing bath, reading a novel and won't be with you for 24 hours').

During the course of working on this book and researching the issues, we've met people who store up lots of extra leave through a timesheet system and then don't take it. Our view is that, except in certain specific circumstances (such as a freelance situation where you have to respond to peaks and troughs in your working year), it's good for the job if you take what leave you can, properly balanced out through the year. The worst scenario is to experience a guilt trip because you believe that by taking your holiday you're letting down your organization. If that's what you feel, you probably need a break more than ever, to get some perspective. Sure, work is important but your organization is not your lover, they will manage without you; and if they really can't they need to look at how they resource your section. Take a break or at the very least, plan to take one soon!

Gordon had a relevant experience when brought in to manage a team producing an innovative and high profile web site. He came on board after the project had started and found that all the key team members had cancelled their leave due to pressure of work. He talked it through with each of them individually and felt that there was a very real dilemma – they desperately needed a break but the project was so tightly scheduled that it would miss its publicly announced deadline if they took those breaks. Clearly, something had gone wrong with the way the project had been set up but the problem was immediate and it looked as though the only way forward was to ask the team to do without their much needed leave. Gordon's solution was to ask them all to book extensive leave for when the project was completed and get this signed off by senior management. Then he worked with each team member to identify some shorter periods – a Friday and Monday, for example – so that they could get away and have some sort of break now. This wasn't the best solution for the project or the team members but it was a workable way forward. Things would have been much better if the team's need for holiday had been properly built into the schedule.

Career breaks

Just as you're at your best in the working day if you can do a variety of tasks, so your working life as a whole will benefit from having some different stimuli and stretching a variety of creative muscles. This might be achieved through changing jobs or shifting and developing roles within jobs. It might be aided by the kinds of things we've been looking at throughout this book – changing the 'how' of work rather than the 'what'.

Another option is to consider a career break. This can be an opportunity to recharge creative batteries, gain some experience in a different (often related) field, and/or to give you a rest, avoiding health problems later on. Many organizations offer help with this kind of scheme. Some actually encourage you to take a long break (say, three months) after ten years' service. Clergy, for example, are encouraged to take a paid sabbatical every ten years, on average. Where a paid sabbatical is not available, arrangements can be made to cover pension contributions and to keep the job open for your return.

Career breaks are not entirely risk-free – many people know the fear that their job might not be there for them when they return – or it might have changed out of all recognition! However, when viewed as part of a life's journey, they can be an important element in achieving goals both within and without the world of work. If you're interested in this option, talk in confidence to those responsible for HR issues in your organization. Perhaps ask them to point you to someone who's done this to get the inside picture.

Go part-time

Consider whether the best way forward for you at the moment is to work less, allowing more time for other things. If you do go part-time, of course, you'll have to cope with less money, but this may be appropriate for a short time while you prioritize other things. People who do this often find it a practical way forward while they consider where they want to go next. One important issue is to think carefully about how you want to use the time, to get the most out of this new opportunity. A good starting point would be to meet with other part-time colleagues and get their take on the advantages and pitfalls. If you decide to take this further, you may need to persuade your manager that it is an option worth considering; see the suggestions for formulating flexible working plans at the start of this chapter.

Take a course – life-long learning

The concept of life-long learning operates on a number of levels:

- keeping your mind active;
- learning new skills;
- topping up knowledge;
- exploring new developments in your field;
- gaining qualifications;
- achieving ambitions;
- exploring areas of interest outside your work.

These days it's easier than ever to embark on a course of study. There's a range of evening classes and distance learning packages available. You can study for a degree with the Open University, or even take an online course with a college in another country. Don't undervalue more practical options such as painting, pottery, learning an instrument or following a drama course. These can be particularly valuable if your work is mainly cerebral.

Good employers are understanding about the demands of learning and the best will encourage you to continually stretch yourself and expand your understanding as in this case study from Rhona:

I had an appraisal with the area manager about a year after I joined the organization. This was arranged after I kicked up a fuss about my workload and what I felt were misrepresentations in the job advert. My team manager was unhappy about this as he felt, quite rightly, that it reflected on him. To my amazement, Robin, my area manager, seemed to understand what I was talking about but his solution seemed crazy – do a business management course on a one-day-a-week basis. Here was I complaining of having too much to do and I thought he understood this, but his solution was to do more – take on a whole course worth of extra work. I tried to dissuade him but he was adamant, saying that the organization needed people like me and he wanted to get the best out of me. He told me to prioritize the course and to start saying no to other things – he'd back me.

To cut a long story short, he was absolutely right. I'm two years into the study now – it could take me another three years to get my degree. I love it. It's given me loads of extra confidence and helped me find new solutions. There are times when it gets really difficult and, at first, my husband didn't like me taking my course books on holiday but I pointed out that he was free to read his bonkbusters while lying on the beach, and I don't mind looking a nerd reading business books in the sun!

And my team manager? I don't think he likes the new me much – he probably knows that I'm after his job, but just as a stepping stone on my way up!

Integrate

We're so used to thinking of work as being a place where one type of activity happens and we think that all the other aspects of our lives need to orbit around this sacred arena. There are good reasons to maintain clear boundaries (see next tip) but if a little integration can make life easier, why not? Let's look at some examples:

- *Shopping.* Shopping and work don't seem to go together – especially with the former becoming more of a leisure activity these days. But there are ways that the more routine grocery shopping can be integrated into work. Internet shopping as offered by the major supermarkets is ideally suited to the workplace. Staff can go online during their lunch break and have their shopping dropped off at work before they leave for home.

Many organizations have formalized this and have an arrangement for the store to make deliveries at set times during the day. Suddenly a big hassle has become painlessly integrated with your job.

If your organization doesn't yet offer this facility, why not suggest it? Point out that from the employer's point of view this is an inexpensive and simple way to buy a lot of goodwill.

- *Keep fit.* Many large organizations have workplace gyms because they recognize their value in keeping staff healthy and in lowering stress. If your organization can't run to this, could they negotiate a special rate with a nearby facility and subsidize membership? How you use the gym would be up to you and the culture of your organization. You could go before or after work, or during a lunch break. Or it could be accepted that, as a valued and trusted task-based worker, you use the gym whenever it suits you and your tasks. Gordon finds that he does a lot of valuable thinking in the gym and always returns to the office refreshed and more productive.
- *Take a (creative) break.* On the whole, you will probably want to keep any creative hobby such as singing, drama, quilting, pottery or writing, separate from work to give you that feeling that this is for you – special, important and personal. However, bringing a creative break into the workspace can be very powerful. It doesn't have to be directly tied to the organization's focus; it could be the opportunity to do something different once a week – a drama class, a dance session, creative games or whatever. This type of creative buzz can have a great effect on the rest of the working day and can free up your thinking to be more creative in the workspace afterwards. Any team-based activity, such as doing drama together, can also pay dividends in team building and socialization at work.
- *Join the club.* Does your workplace offer club facilities such as sporting teams, a theatre club, bar facilities, and so on? If so, these can provide a stress-busting antidote to work pressures – especially if you thrash your boss at squash! Or, of course, work with her to lead the softball team to victory.

The other practical advantage of work-based clubs is their convenience – if you were going to join a choir anyway, it might

be advantageous to join one that you can visit direct from
with no travel. Of course, you might prefer not to mix wor
leisure in this way and our next tip concerns this.

Boundaries

We've found the setting of clear boundaries to be crucial. This is
mainly because Ronni's vocation can be all-enveloping, non-stop
seven days and seven nights a week. There are a number of issues
wrapped up in this. One vicar friend, for example, believes that total
integration of her life and her work is the ideal. She doesn't want
boundaries because her concept of her vocation is all about the
person she is rather than the tasks she does. Thinking in this way
works for her, but we've found tensions between the roles of priest
and parent, vicar and wife, individual and official. For us the way
forward has been about setting boundaries – sometimes quite rigid
ones. Examples are:

- not being available during the early evening so that we can eat and
  be together as a family;
- trying to protect one day off a week;
- trying to limit the number of evening meetings;
- booking in occasional Saturdays as an extra day off when the
  family can do something together.

The traffic hasn't all been one way. Gordon has adjusted his working
life to take on more childcare responsibilities and generally leaves
work earlier than colleagues to allow him to get home before Ronni
goes out in the evening, and to allow for eating together when
possible.

You're not a vicar – so what's all this to do with you? You'll still
need to think about boundaries, particularly if you work at home at
all and live with the potential for confusion of home/work space.
You might also find it useful to think of your job in terms of a
vocation – perhaps, like our friend, you and your work role are
closely intertwined. Certainly, many artists think of themselves in
this way and it may be an important aspect of the future of work,
helping us to break down rigid views of when and where work
happens.

Whatever your work, however it's organized, we think that the
key message is to be aware of the boundaries issues for you and, as

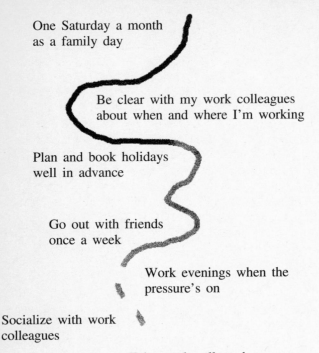

One Saturday a month
as a family day

Be clear with my work colleagues
about when and where I'm working

Plan and book holidays
well in advance

Go out with friends
once a week

Work evenings when the
pressure's on

Socialize with work
colleagues

Take work calls at home

far as possible, take control so that you set the boundaries and create space for what matters to you.

A useful exercise might be to map out the boundaries between your work and other aspects of your life. Draw it as a map, with the different aspect separated by heavy lines for rigid boundaries, lighter lines for boundaries that can be allowed to drift occasionally, dotted lines for flexible boundaries and no line for places where work and life merge.

When you've drawn your map as it is at present, make changes so that it reflects how you'd like it to operate in the future, then set some targets for making a difference. There's an example of a map shown above.

Here are some further examples of boundary setting and how it's worked out in practice for a number of people:

Film action

Hari and Daphne are busy professionals who instigated some counselling to try to keep some focus on the importance of their relationship, which seemed to be pushed out by the demands of their jobs, children and caring for his parents. The counsellor suggested that they revive what had brought them together – a love of theatre. This proved impractical because going to the theatre regularly involved a 30-mile trip and a late return. They switched their focus to early-evening showings at the local cinema and now leave work by 4.00 one day every couple of weeks to see a film together. A small sacrifice in terms of working hours (both work too long anyway), and a bit of organization have made a big difference to their marriage which, as noted elsewhere, will also be good for their work. As their counsellor pointed out, they enjoy going to the cinema together and, by making time in this way they are clearly saying to each other how important their relationship is.

Drinking partners

When Julie started a new job in a new area, she was quickly assimilated into her work team – a team that had a strong social ethos which embraced going for a drink after work on a number of occasions and monthly social events. Although she was initially grateful for this, over time she began to resent it, and finally plucked up courage to say to her boss, in confidence, that she liked her colleagues but didn't feel that she had to be friends with them; she didn't think it was necessary to spend so much social time together. Her boss didn't really understand and felt slighted, saying that she was proud of the cohesion of the team and that the social aspect was important. Julie chose to stick with it, because the work was important to her. In time she reached a balance – sometimes declining the offer to go for a drink, sometimes accepting – and Julie's colleagues learnt to respect her, both as a colleague in work time and as someone with other priorities out of working hours. For Julie, the setting of boundaries was a fluid and developing process, involving give and take, developing as she proved her worth and demonstrated her personal qualities.

Singing manager

Clare, a senior manager with the BBC, has a love of singing and belongs to a choir. In order to make weekly choir practice she has to leave work by 5.00 sharp on Mondays. Her job involves many high-level meetings and it can be hard to hit her Monday deadline. She's proud of the fact that over a five-year period she's only had to miss her practice twice. For her it's a give and take situation with the bias very much towards her choir commitments on that one day a week. Clare finds the physical, mental and aesthetic engagement of singing the perfect complement to her senior manager role, making her a better and more confident manager, and a more rounded person.

Consider your physical, mental and spiritual needs

So far we've simplified lifestyle choices by thinking in terms of a balance between life and work as if these are two ends of the scales pivoted around some notional sense of 'you'. This is a good model for thinking about the issues but as we all know things are more complicated than this and different aspects of being a balanced, healthy individual intermesh with one another and with your work and non-work commitments. If, for example, your work is strenuous and keeps you fit, you may not need to go to the gym in your non-work time. If your work feeds your artistic and spiritual side, you may want to spend more of your non-work time on physical pursuits. So alongside your work–life balance as this book has been considering it, you might like to make an audit of your mental, spiritual, creative and physical needs. Ask yourself where these needs are met – at work, away from work, or both. Thinking about work in this way can be useful when considering a new job or developing what you currently do.

We've already looked at integrating keep fit and physical training into the working day. We've suggested how you might build in creative breaks. You might also want to consider finding a time of quiet for contemplation, meditation or prayer. Most anti-stress counsellors now recognize the value of these kinds of activities and there is evidence to suggest that they can be powerful components in a balanced approach to work. Finding time for a STEP exercise each day might revolutionize how you see yourself and your work – or it might just give you a bit of break. Either is useful!

Listening to dreams, friends, prayer and inner voices

Underpinning much of this book has been the notion of stepping back, thinking and meditating on your situation – seeking clarity on how you can change things. An important part of this is listening to those around you, to yourself and, if you have a spiritual belief, to your journeying in prayer.

Listen to yourself

What do you really think about your work–life balance? What are your inner voices telling you? Here are some ways to find out.

Literally listen to yourself – take note of what you say about your job when talking to others. What do your comments and attitudes reveal? What are you really saying beneath what you're saying? Here's an example from Oona who works in HR:

I realized that I always spoke about work negatively when out with friends, even though I quite enjoy it most of the time. I was in a groove of negativity because everyone else was moaning about their work. So I stopped talking in this way and tried to say what I really thought. In doing so, I discovered that I'd actually been giving my work too high a priority, blaming it for mood swings and mild depression that were really nothing to do with work but more to do with some unresolved issues in my personal life. For a while I chose to see work as something that I did, not something that defined me – and this was really useful.

Listen to your dreams

Learn to recall your dreams as you wake up. Can any of them be interpreted as being about work? How do work colleagues and tasks appear? What happened to them and what happened to you in the dream? Think about the symbols and actions of the dreams – what do they tell you? Here's one of Gordon's work dreams:

I dreamt that I was on a water ride at a theme park. A cameraman who I'd worked with recently was in the boat with me. We just sat back and chatted as the boat followed its own course.

The presence of the cameraman set this dream clearly in the work context. Gordon had been worrying about some uncertainty in his job and had been looking around for other opportunities. In the dream, his subconscious seemed to be balancing this by saying – it's okay, just relax and enjoy the ride; you'll get there just the same.

There are many theories of dream interpretation and this is too complex an area to be covered by this book, but you might find it useful to listen to your dreams as they reveal concerns and questions about your work. There are lots of books on dream interpretation if you're interested in exploring this further.

Inner voices

Like Joan of Arc we all hear voices – memories, the voice of conscience or our own voice as we rehearse what we're going to say. It's a good idea to collect your thoughts every so often, perhaps at the end of the day. Run through the different inner voices you've heard. You may ask, *What have these voices been saying to me?* But it might be better to ask, *What have I been saying to me?* An example of this might be a memory of a vocation you were once determined to follow, perhaps as a child. Many people want to pursue glamorous lifestyles, perhaps as a famous actor, or as a singer. Sometimes those voices can still whisper failure unless we're able to recognize them for what they are and realize that we've matured now and our childhood self has no right to brand us in that way. This can be more difficult if the voice is a memory of a parent who we feel is disappointed in how we've turned out. Again, we're getting into deep waters here and paddling beyond the scope of this book. The key message is to be aware of what we are saying to and about ourselves and to be able to respond in a mature way. If you find that your inner voices are holding you back, leading you to live with a sense of failure, you might like to meet with a counsellor to talk this through – perhaps talk it out. Many employers offer a discreet counselling service – they pay but don't know who's using the service or what the issues are. Alternatively, your doctor may be able to refer you, particularly if the issue shows signs of affecting your physical or mental health.

Here's what Donald, who works in consultancy, had to say after three sessions with a counsellor:

I was extremely sceptical about the role of counselling. I went, on the recommendation of my doctor, about three years ago, and felt that the whole process was a waste of time – we just never seemed to get to the bottom of things. A couple of months ago I found that I was getting really angry about something at work, to the extent that I threw things across the room and my wife became anxious because she was never sure what mood I'd be in when I got home. Eventually she persuaded me to try again and I arranged to use the counselling service provided through my office. It took a lot of courage to phone the first time – I went out of the building and used my mobile so that I wouldn't be overheard.

In fact, after a little hesitancy I found it a great relief to start talking a
my problems and I began looking forward to the next time. I guess th.
just clicked with this counsellor and was unlucky three years ago. I'll miss
going every week, but I couldn't justify any more time on it now because
I've made some real progress and learned some useful strategies for coping
with stress. One of the best things is knowing that this service is there so I
can pick up the phone and make an appointment if I need to again.

Prayer

Prayer is intensely personal, bringing us into contact with our
innermost core of beliefs. It also means different things to different
people; some believe it is very like a two-way and personal
conversation with God. For others prayer is less defined and is about
tuning in to mystery, and there is clearly a cross-over with
meditation here. Prayer may seem a long way form the practical
concerns of this book, but our starting point involves balancing and
considering all the aspects of life, and your spiritual journey is very
much part of this.

Whatever your specific focus, some people and faiths build a
disciplined prayer life into their daily routine including work. When
we lived in Nottingham the staff of our local corner shop would be
prostrate on the floor facing Mecca at certain times of the day – it
did us good to wait patiently until they could serve us.

Most people find prayer difficult but worthwhile and find value in
bringing their whole life, including work, before that which is
greater and other than themselves.

Mental modelling

Neural Linguistic Programming (NLP) is a theory about how we all
see (model) the world differently and how we can use this to be
aware of and, to some extent, control, our mental states. One
technique is to alter your thoughts and feelings by thinking about a
time when these were different. For example, if you have to give a
talk or presentation and you feel uneasy, not mentally prepared for it,
think about a time when you gave a good talk. How did it feel? What
mental state were you in? The theory is that thinking about a
previous 'healthy' state will help you to recreate it. Many people
have found this a useful way forward and its connections with a
healthy work–life balance are obvious.

There is, of course, a great deal more to NLP than this, and you'll find a number of books about it in the education, training or management sections of bookshops and libraries. It might be for you and help you change how you think and feel.

Key issues

In this chapter we've looked at practical steps you can take to change how and when you work, and how you can integrate work and the rest of your life. We've looked at:

- Identifying where your time and energy is currently focused.
- Identifying what you can change.
- Formulating action plans.
- Childcare facilities.
- Parents' groups.
- Flexibility policies.
- Self-organizing teams.
- Career breaks.
- Life-long learning.
- Internet shopping.
- Going to the gym.
- Creative breaks.
- Workplace clubs.
- Setting boundaries.
- Listening to others, dreams, prayer, inner voices.

Why not take a look back at your list of indicators of who you are and why you are interested in these issues from Chapter 1? Can any of these practical suggestions help you to meet your objectives?

4

Relationships in balance

One of the biggest motivators for the sudden interest in work–life balance is change in working patterns. As explored in Chapter 1:

- in many relationships both partners work;
- caring responsibilities for young and old are increasingly complex;
- work is more fractured with less 9–5 and five-days-a-week working.

All of this impacts on the world of work, but we believe that it is most keenly felt in the home, and in the space between people – the committed relationships that are the foundation of society. Relationships have borne the brunt of change, sometimes providing an airbag of safety, or often a crumple zone when things hit head on. Sometimes, though, relationships are tested to destruction by the pressures of work.

This chapter gave us the biggest headache when thinking about addressing you, our audience, because we're writing about personal things – relationships, attitudes and home life. We're bound to have got it wrong. We talk a lot about partners but you might not have one, or you might be just beginning a relationship. The same might apply to children or elderly relatives or pets (one of Gordon's colleagues cried for days on end when her rabbit died – this was something that really mattered to her). In the end we decided that we simply couldn't cover all the bases from gerbils to grannies and back again, so take what you can, and if we tread on your toes by not mentioning your significant relationship or overdoing it on someone else's, sorry.

Elsewhere we've looked at how you can seek to change attitudes and patterns of work; in this chapter we want to look at practical steps you can take within relationships, but this shouldn't be your only line of attack. Work–life balance requires a change at work as well, so use the ideas in this section in conjunction with the rest of the book. This shouldn't be seen as a stand-alone chapter because you can't stand alone on this issue. The world of work is changing too and will change further as the impact of these issues begins to bite.

It's said that 'continental' people work to live, while Brits live to work. Earlier in the book, we encouraged you to think about what *you* work for. Use the following exercise to establish your attitude towards *your partner's* work:

How do you feel about your partner's work? Take a look at these statements:

I'm proud of my partner and his or her work.
I'm happy that my partner is happy in his or her work.
I'm worried about the amount of time and energy my partner gives to his or her work.
I'm jealous of the time and energy my partner gives to his or her work.
I hate the demands that my partner's job makes on him or her.
I'm happy about my partner's job but I wish it left more time for us.
My partner's job is breaking up our relationship.
I wish I had my partner's job.
I wish my partner had a job.

Do any of these apply to you? Take a moment to complete this sentence for yourself. My partner's job makes me feel . . .

Now the hard part; find some time to talk through these issues with your partner. If you find that difficult, see 'Talk' below.

Here's an example from real life:

James writes:
One major problem that we've identified is that I tended to over-react to the problems and issues that Olive's teaching job threw up.

When she went to Governors' meetings I stayed at home (because of caring responsibilities) and worried – these meetings have been quite tricky and upsetting in the past.

I worried about what kind of state she'd be in when she got home. I worried about hurtful things that may have been said to her. Also, if I'm honest, I worried about what she may say in return and the repercussions that this might bring.

So we had a problem that was directly related to work–life balance – Olive's work, our life and my lack of balance. My worry may have been understandable, but was it practical and did it help? I had to face the fact that my worrying didn't really help – didn't help Olive or me. It didn't make any difference to her difficulties, it was not practical and I suspect it was not supportive. And there's something worse; I came to realize that it demonstrated a lack of trust, an over-protectiveness, a need to stick my nose into things that weren't really my business.

The way forward was for me to change, to step back and realize that I could be more supportive by being less involved.

The above is one of those situations where realizing the problem went a long way to solving it, and things were much better once James made this analysis and acted on it. But we need to be clear that there's no magic wand and this wasn't a simple matter for James to put right. Many relationship issues grow out of deeply ingrained attitudes – they can become focused on the character and personal style of an individual and, because of this, you may find that help is needed to unpick the complexities. As mentioned in the above example, you can start by stepping back and understanding, and here a third person can be useful. Arranging to see a counsellor, or talking with a trusted friend together isn't a sign of weakness or that your relationship is in trouble – rather, it can represent a commitment to growing and changing together. Whatever you do, and however you tackle these kinds of issues we strongly recommend two things: reflect on the situation, and talk together about it.

Reflecting

As we've said elsewhere, one of the most intractable difficulties of untangling work–life balance issues is their complexity. In many of our lives, there's simply too much going on and all of it is important. As you start to think about relationships and work–life balance, give yourself time to stop and think. We've devoted a section of this book to reflective exercises, imaginative and creative ways to help you to do the following:

Step back – review your situation from a more distant perspective.
Take a different view – look at what *you* could change.
Envision – a different future, where things are more in balance.
Prioritize – to begin to make that future a reality.

We've tried to provide options to pick and choose from so that you can find an imaginative way of thinking about these issues that's right for you.

Talk

As we're talking here about relationships, in most cases thinking and reflecting will lead on to talking. So before you make changes to your lifestyle(s), make time to *talk* about making changes to your lifestyles. We've found, along with most couples, that not talking about an issue, any issue, is the first step to its becoming a problem and, as we've seen elsewhere, problems are part of the definition of a relationship. They can lead to opportunities for growth and change or they can become obstacles. Move on those problems early to keep your work and life as balanced as possible.

You've read the above and you're thinking – sure, make time, like I've got all the time in the world to talk about this and every other issue! I'm reading this steaming pile of amateur philosophizing on a crowded train, late for work where I've got too much to do. There's a mountain of ironing sitting at home and when I get back late tonight I'll be too tired to think about talking, let alone talking about radical lifestyle changes and as for actually doing anything . . . please! My life is too crowded, stretched and hassled. I want solutions, not a requirement for yet more things to fill time.

Hmm, thanks for the endorsement! If your thoughts line up with the above statement, perhaps look at it this way: whatever your views on any sort of afterlife, you only have one life as the person you are now in the world you're in now. What you will be can wait. What do you want from this life, what's important now? If your relationship is important to you, then surely you have to think issues through and talk about them with your partner. If you're too busy to take the time for this – you're too busy. Find time, any time, to do the thinking – travelling time, chores time, just before bedtime; and make time for the talking. Here's how one couple created time for that all-important communication:

We *are* very busy. I know everyone says that but Phil's job means he often has to work in the evenings, I commute and arrive home late and frazzled, there are childcare and eldercare responsibilities. But we've made choices and we're determined to make our relationship work so we instigated talk night. Here's how it works, but it's so simple really! Every Thursday night we make sure we go to bed early which means about 10.00 for us and we don't read or anything else, we just lie there holding hands and talk about anything that's concerning us. It could be really trivial – I told Phil once that

I was resentful of the way that he seemed to take things for granted and never said thank you – for example. Or it can be more important, perhaps work related such as talking about frustrations in our jobs and how they affect us at home. Talking at a regular time every week has been good for us, I'm sure, and has led to some practical outcomes. One of the most far-reaching has been that Phil has managed to reduce the number of evenings he has to work. We've also instigated quite formal diary sessions when we work out who's in when and who will cover certain tasks and events. It's not a panacea and there are definitely times when the conversation is stilted – either because we're cross with each other and not ready to talk or because we're just too tired; but at least there's an opportunity to talk and that little bit of structure has been very important for us.

Communication is the medium of any relationship, so here are some more suggestions for how to make time for talking:

- Set the alarm and wake up early – have a cup of tea, coffee or what you will and talk for 15 minutes before the start of the day. This won't work if you're on different shifts – in that situation you could make it a priority to fix things so that you can be in together occasionally. Nor is it likely to work if you've a young child or two who always manage to wake up before you; and anyway, in that situation, you probably need as much sleep as possible.
- Drop something to make time to talk. You could drop a TV programme or sex, or an office social, for example. Cancelling something that matters to you to make time to talk demonstrates that this is important to you, and that can go a long way towards resolving areas of conflict.
- Make a phone date and phone each other, perhaps from work, at set times. Find a quiet and private place to talk on the phone.

We recommend face-to-face talking wherever possible, with a phone call as a good alternative. Leaving notes or communicating by email might work for you but there is a danger that it can be impersonal and things can easily be misinterpreted without the inflexions of speech to oil difficult communications. That being said, there is value in writing to each other alongside, or as a preparation for, talking. Sometimes you can put different things in a letter and compose your thoughts more carefully. Some people find they can be more informal or even daring in a note.

Here are some thoughts that a STEP session and/or talking together might throw up,

I'm way out of balance here, my job is too demanding and it's damaging my important relationships. I have to change jobs or stop working.

Deep breath – this is the big one! It might be hard to come to this conclusion; it will probably be even harder to do something about it. The following may help:

- Give it time; repeat the STEP exercise and talk about it again in a week or so, to help you be sure that this is the right conclusion.
- Look again at Chapter 2. Can you stay with your job but change how it works for you and how you work for it? Could you consider part-time working?
- Try to untangle your feelings about this. Is it *this* job that's the problem, or any job? Is this really about relationships or is it that you want to follow a completely different path? Perhaps you want to go to Hollywood or join a commune! Don't knock it if you do, just be clear about the decisions you make and why you make them.
- Talk it through with as many trusted friends as you can, but guard against this becoming the sort of 'moan' about work that we all indulge in from time to time – be focused, realistic and practical.
- Choose the right moment to discuss this with your partner, especially if it's a big money issue for you both.
- Weigh up, as best you can, what you'll be giving up if you leave your current job – money, office friendships, routine, for example. Balance these against the relationship gains.
- Think through the effects on your partner, trying to understand his or her point of view. Might your giving up a particular job close down options for him or her?

My job seems to make my partner angry, and I resent that. My job is important to me – why should I just fit in with my partner's lifestyle?

This is one of those areas where the strength and style of your relationship will be important as you try to move forward. As ever, we're going to base any suggestions on that all-important word – TALK. In fact that's our only suggestion – make time to talk, explain, consider the other person's point of view. Some people say that they don't have time to talk, but if you can't find the time, you're not in a relationship. See suggestions under 'Talk' on page 58.

We both like a good deal of our work, but we just can't fit everything in and this is putting real pressure on our relationship.

It's not the individual jobs that are the problem here, it's the combination of both partners' work and all the other important aspects of your lives. Some suggestions for thinking and talking through this issue are given below, but also look at the next section – Sex, chores and rock-n-roll – for some specific relationship factors you could change:

- In as objective a way as possible, talk through how healthy you feel your relationship is. Try not to take a snapshot view, but consider over a period of time to get a more balanced perspective. If the various factors crowding into your life mean that the relationship itself is in danger, then agree that you have to take action if you want your relationship to thrive.
- Analyse all the elements that fill your crowded life, with particular emphasis on prioritizing. Are there any areas that could take a back seat for a while?
- Write to yourself – send yourself a letter setting out the issues as you see them. This is a great way to clarify your thinking before talking with your partner. You can also send yourself a letter to be opened in a month's time as a record of how you hope things will change.
- Don't allow yourself to think that nothing can change. If the things that really matter to you are under threat – relationships, health, a future for your children, for example; if these are in danger because of your work–life balance, then something *has* to change. Be prepared to say no (see Chapter 2), to disappoint some people, be prepared to take some flak. These are life-story issues and nothing is more important.

Children

We've focused mainly on adult relationships and partnerships, but clearly where children are involved all these issues take on an extra dimension. We're not childcare experts, we're just parents who have muddled through, meeting the challenges as they came along. We're living with adolescent children for the first time now, just as in the past we had babies, toddlers and school-age children – all for the first time. So we're reluctant to offer advice in this area because meddling by well-intentioned amateurs could be unhelpful (but are there any professional parents?). You know best what your children need and how their needs will best fit into your overall work–life balance. That said here are a few thoughts that our experience has shaped up.

There's a lot of pressure put upon parents when thinking about work–life balance and children. It's important to put all that on one side. Be clear what *you* believe is best for your children. For example, we really value the experiences with other children that ours gained through time at child minders. We equally valued the fact that they could start state nursery at the age of three. We gave our children these experiences because they were practical and we felt they would be good for the children's development. Not everyone agreed or agrees with us. These are decisions that we took, laying aside societal and other pressures – you might take a different view. Parents should proceed on the basis of *their* principles, not peer or societal pressure.

Now they're older, we've found it helpful to bring our children into discussions about job changes and other lifestyle decisions. Here's an example of this, from another clergy couple:

Richard was recently thinking about a new job in the Church. It had a number of things that seemed important: it used his education and development skills, it had a nice house in a nice location and it offered quite a bit more money! Initial thoughts were – go for it, Rich! But as we discussed it as a family, one aspect became a real sticking point – an absolute requirement for Morning Prayer at 7.00 every morning, Monday to Saturday inclusive, with a later start at 8.00 on Sunday. There were some practical reasons for this, but our children suspected it was pretty much to do with a church unwilling to move with the times and admit that taking priests away from their families at the start of the day could be counter-productive. We talked it through and all decided the price wasn't worth it. This was not so much to do with the actual times as the attitude that it suggested toward family life. It's also part of the catching up that the Church has to do now that it has women ministers. It's not that it's a bad thing to drag *mothers* away from the family unnecessarily at odd hours:

we're clear as a family that it's a bad thing to drag *parents* away from the family unnecessarily, and men haven't been good at standing up to this sort of thing.

In the end, the message has to be to add your children's needs into all your work–life balance thinking. In partnerships the only way forward is to share equally in the burdens and joys of being parents. Gordon, for example, did a fair bit of working at home in order to be around at the end of the school day when the children were younger. This wasn't always ideal from a work perspective but sometimes work has to give a little, just as at other times the family or partner has to do the giving. As the children grow up, this balance will change. There may be no easy answers, but a good start is to be clear about the issues and your aims with yourself, your partner and your children.

Sex, chores and rock-n-roll

We're not Nancy Friday, Mrs Beeton or Elvis, but here are our thoughts on muddling through in these areas where an unhealthy work–life balance can play havoc with relationships.

Intimacy

If you've been flicking through this book and your eye just happens to have alighted on this section – welcome!

As a very young man and in what seems like a different life in an alternative universe (but was in fact a period of relative religious fundamentalism), Gordon once read a book about relationships written by a vicar. He eagerly turned straight to the chapter on sex and discovered a sort of manual rather like a DIY book – fix here, glue there, hammer this bit. Although it was all about parts of the body and things to do with them, it was equally explicit. We apologise, but you won't get that here. There are plenty of books that will give you that sort of advice but what we're concerned about are those perennial themes of this book:

- What's important?
- How do you balance your time?
- How do you balance your energies?

- How can you find the right home for all kinds of intimacy within your relationship, within your own and your partner's work–life balance?

The rest, be it MFI, Habitat, Ikea or home-made ironwork, is your affair. The central focus of this section is about finding time for intimacy – whatever form that takes for you. It can include physicality of course, but it also embraces tenderness, talking together and simply being together.

When you get to the prioritizing part, you'll probably face some difficult decisions. Assuming you've thought through the options and discussed them with your partner, here are some possible ways forward. As ever, they may not be easy, and they may not fit your situation without some adjustment but we hope they'll help.

You've decided that you and your partner need to make more time to be together. How can you do it?

- You might choose to work less, but first check out the working smarter suggestions in Chapter 2.
- Be organized. Agree some possible times and write them on a calendar (in code if necessary – MFI or Ikea?). Be clear with each other that you don't have to stick to these times – mood and hormones might come into it after all! Overbook to allow for last-minute cancellations.
- Don't let being organized stifle your spontaneity or creativity – allow at least a little space for impulsive behaviour.
- Agree that your relationship is important enough for other areas of your work–life balance story to flex around it. This might mean in practice that you'll leave a social event early in order to make time to be together, or that you'll miss an important meeting. This might cause you and other people some problems but it might be right in the light of your overall work–life balance.
- Build in an understanding of each other's moods and tiredness factors. Look at different times of the day and night to suit both partners – perhaps set the alarm early. After all, you'd get up early if it were important for your job.

One partner feels that the other's work–life story is out of balance in this area. You've talked and hit an impasse. This happens to many couples after the birth of a child, for example, when tiredness, hormones and a sudden change of lifestyle knock everything for six, particularly sex. The phrase 'an early night' takes on a new and more prosaic meaning. In this and situations like it, you might just have to accept that you're in a low sex phase of your life. It's important, but so is your sanity and so is your new baby or new job, or caring responsibilities. We believe that you can 'have it all', we're committed to 'life in all its fullness' – we just recognize that it might not all be possible at the same time! Perhaps all that can be said is the patronising – it will change. One practical step you can take is to set a time to talk about this again, put a date in the diary for three weeks' time and keep talking at regular intervals until the situation changes and you can start to move intimacy of all kinds up the priority list again. Try to keep some form of intimacy alive – a quick and personal talk each day, for example.

And while you're in the midst of a low sex phase, if throwing this book across the room helps . . .

Any more detail here is outside the scope of this book, but where it really is felt that work–life balance is key to the disharmony in the relationship you might like to think about the following:

- It can be hard to be objective in the midst of churned-up emotions, feelings of rejection and disappointment. Try to get some sense of perspective, of understanding where each of you is in relation to the issue.
- Try to untangle the important part that sex plays in your relationship from other factors such as feeling appreciated, valued and loved. It can be dangerous to feel that these things can only be expressed in one way.
- Independently work through a STEP exercise, focusing on issues of intimacy in your work–life balance story, then talk through your discoveries together.
- In some circumstances, and depending on the nature of your relationship and how easily you communicate with each other, you may feel that you need to talk these issues through with an independent 'facilitator', possibly a trusted friend, more likely a professional counsellor.
- However you decide to go forward, don't leave it. Sooner is better than later because if these issues are not tackled, they can be very damaging to your relationship.

You both feel that a period of celibacy is the best way forward. Some practical suggestions are:

- Be sure that you feel that the pressures of work (or whatever else is driving this decision) are really worth it. Are you doing this for good work–life balance reasons, or are you allowing work too high a priority because of peer pressure? (See Chapter 2.)
- Be clear what you're talking about, making sure that you've both signed up to the same ground rules.
- Set a time limit and set a date and time to assess how it's working.

Chores

How dull, after all that sex in the last section, to be talking about chores. By definition most people hate chores and find them . . . a chore! They are boring, time-consuming, frustrating and annoying, and a real cause in stress in relationships – so rich pickings for this book.

We're talking about household tasks here – washing, ironing, nappy-changing, cooking, washing up, dusting, vacuuming, and so on. Of course there are chores at work too, but they fall into a different category and can be mopped up through some of the changes suggested in Chapter 2.

However dull these household chores are, they're essential – we need clean clothes, food, clean plates to eat off, and so on. So what's important here? Let's start by recognizing that:

- Chores are necessary.
- Chores take time away from other important and fun things.
- Chores cause stress in relationships.
- Chores are low glamour and probably not in the least career-enhancing (butlers and cleaners may demur).
- Not everyone finds all chores totally boring – they can provide a welcome break from brain work and give space for meditation, prayer or gently ruminating.

And let's set our basic assumptions:

- If you can afford to pay other people to do all your chores, you can skip this section.
- Different people have different standards. Ronni's very diligent

about washing and putting out the recycling; Gordon has a good line about the jury still being out on the scientific case for it.

- Although they sound like a joke, chores can be a cause of strong resentment in relationships and form an integral part of most people's work–life balance story.

Here's what a couple of our friends say about chores:

Jane writes: There are times when I get fed up with being the one who's left at home to take the dog out, empty the dishwasher, empty the tumble drier, empty the washing machine, put the washing away, feed the cat and dog . . . It's a pressure due to John's work that I really resent.

John writes: There are times when I get fed up with being the one who's left at home to take the dog out, empty the dishwasher, empty the tumble drier, empty the washing machine, put the washing away, feed the cat and dog . . . It's a pressure due to Jane's work that I really resent.

Note that in the above, it is not so much the chores themselves as the feeling of resentment at being the partner who does the most. If it's a man/woman thing, then some might say that as women have a centuries long start over men in this area, it's up to men to take over the whole show and do a bit of catching up. There's some justice there, but only if you can live life seeing the bigger picture, with a global, historical view as your perspective. Most of us live on a smaller scale and anyway, one thing we're very clear on is that we don't want to add ammunition to the battle of the sexes. That being so, here are some practical thoughts about chores:

- Use a STEP exercise to gain some perspective. Sort out where practical issues end and emotional ones begin. Identify where chores are getting in the way of your relationship and/or damaging your work–life balance.
- Start by agreeing with your partner that you're looking for an equal spread of tasks here – don't accept 'but I do all the car repairs', unless week by week they really do balance other chores (and if they do, perhaps we're moving away from 'chore' here and into hobby?).
- Forget new man, new age, and new millennium – just think about new gadgets. If you can afford a tumble drier, dishwasher, and robot vacuum cleaner, why haven't you got them?

- Farm out anything you can afford to. There are cleaning and ironing services, for example. Don't feel guilty about spending money on these things, think of it as job creation! Also see this as a work–life balance issue; one reason for working is to get money to use in exactly this way to give you time for other things that matter to you.
- Recognize that one person's chore (cooking, for example), might be another person's relaxation. Gordon bumped into a colleague in the gym who confessed that he enjoyed washing up – a nice mindless task with a single clear focus and a definite end point. Alas, folks, he's in a relationship but keep your eyes open, there could be someone out there who likes vacuuming!
- Be hard-nosed and practical – these are things you have to do in order to do other things that you want to do. Grab the bull by the horns and sort it out! Work through it with your partner.
- Be prepared to learn new skills, see below!

Gordon writes: After a few years of doing my bit, laundry is still a total mystery to me. It's an area ripe for some genius to sort out. Among its more impenetrable ambiguities are:

- Why can't everything go in the tumble drier?
- Why is the little label with helpful symbols designed so that it washes out and can't be read?
- Why are shirts impossible to iron?
- Why are there so many pairs of almost (but not quite) identical black socks?
- Why don't we all move somewhere warm and become naturists?

No easy answers here then, and we don't want to turn this book into the sort of gadget catalogue with enticing blurbs for labour-saving devices:

Why not give everyone's black socks their own distinctive smell? It's easy to do and won't wash out. Sorting socks is a breeze when you know that two cabbages go together and both go in Laura's drawer.

The best advice is that given above; see this as a work–life balance issue and make changes where you can. You've nothing to lose but your deep relationship with white goods.

Rock-n-roll

We know that rock-n-roll was originally a descriptive term for sex, but we're using it to represent play and fun, or, if you prefer, leisure activities. In many ways, these go to the heart of the work–life balance question, forcing us to ask, do we live to work or work to live?

If you have any answers at all to this kind of philosophizing, they're likely to be conditioned by the type of work you do. Ronni loves being a vicar, though she doesn't equally embrace all aspects of how it works in practice. Gordon gets a real buzz out of making a Radio 4 drama, or working on a BBC Education Website, but he doesn't get that same high from all aspects of his work. For both of us there are times when work is the most fulfilling thing we can do, and times when it's a pain that gets in the way of other important parts of our lives. In an ideal work–life balance situation for couples you'd find:

- enough time to do some fun and creative things together;
- time for each partner to explore his or her own interests;
- each partner finding challenge and interest in their work;
- leisure interests feeding into work by providing rest, relaxation and a sense of perspective.

If this is how it works for you, read no further. In fact, write your own book on the subject and share your secret with a waiting world.

The fact is that, for most of us, finding time to fit everything in is a struggle and it's often the relaxing and fun part of our lives that gets squeezed. It's easier to give up a hobby than to change the way you work, and it's often easier to deny your relationship needs than to say no to your boss.

In fact, having a challenging, enjoyable and fulfilling life outside of work has enormous benefits for you and for your work. Many companies recognize that it's in their interests to employ and nurture people who have a vibrant life outside of work.

There is such a wide range of fun and leisure activities that we'll confine ourselves to some general principles and exercises. First, do a quick hours count of the time you spend in an average week:

- at work;

- engaged in leisure activities with your partner;
- engaged in leisure activities on your own or with a different group of people.

If you have the time and interest, you could try the de luxe version of this where you keep a diary or log of your activities over a period, say, two weeks. Ronni did this once and it proved extremely useful in assessing her workload. In her case, for example, it demonstrated that she was spending over 40 per cent of her time in administration meetings. This was due to the convoluted structure of her job, but it wasn't actually what her vocation is about and much of it was 'self-feeding' – one meeting led to another which led to another. She used this information to put a stop to some of it and thus free up more time for other things, including leisure.

We can't suggest what a healthy balance would be in terms of your time – that all depends on the kind of person you are and what you do, although we would suggest that a healthy work–life balance will include all three elements above. Take a look at the results for yourself. Do they tell you anything?

Now take a look at it in a different way. Think in terms of 'energies'. This is where our science-minded readers close the book (if they haven't already!), and those of you into New Age religions start to pay attention. In fact, by 'energies' we mean things that enliven and engage you, things that give you a buzz and a sense of fulfilment. The point is, as mentioned above, that sometimes work can give that buzz and, sadly, leisure can be a bore! Look again at your hour count, above, and try to analyse it in terms of energies (give a percentage 'energize' grade to each activity). Does this tell a different story to the straight hours count?

Now think though any changes you can make to increase those areas of your life that gives you an energetic buzz, and reduce those that don't. You could use a STEP imagination exercise, once again, to help you think it through. You might also find the prioritizing and time creation ideas under 'Intimacy' (page 63) can be usefully applied here.

Finally, some questions to help you think through the issues raised in this chapter:

- If, on a trip to a parallel universe I could only take with me my work or my leisure activities, which would I take?

70

- When I introduce myself to strangers do I define myself in terms of my job or my relationships?
- What one change would do the most to improve the balance between my relationships and work?
- What word or phrase best sums up my attitude to the effect of work on my relationships?
- If I lost my job tomorrow, what would I most miss?
- Which of these could I most easily change to create more time for the others – intimacy, chores, rock and roll?
- Who is a good role model for me in this area?
- To which do I give the most energy – work or my relationships?
- Am I going to change something, starting now? What will it be?

Key issues

- Take the long view – what's the ideal balance for your relationships (including children) and work?
- What is the effect of your partner's job on you, and your job on your partner?
- TALK – make time to communicate regularly.
- Consider the place of your children in your work – life balance story. Be clear on your principles.
- Think about the importance of intimacy in your relationship and decide when and how to prioritize it.
- Look at the division of labour in relation to chores – get rid of what you can!
- Do you live to work or work to live? Look at leisure – with your partner, with others/solitary?
- Take a time audit and an 'energies audit' of your leisure time.
- Finally, KEEP TALKING!

5
STEP back

Throughout this book we've regularly referred to the idea of STEP exercises:

Step back – review your situation from a more distant perspective.
Take a different view – look at what *you* could change.
Envision – a different future, where things are more in balance.
Prioritize – to begin to make that future a reality.

In this section we want to give you some ideas on how to do this. Our suggestions range from the boringly obvious to the ridiculously bizarre – or maybe they're not way out enough for you. It all depends on who you are and how you like to think about things. We hope there's something for everyone and if any of it seems too far-gone for you – we hope it at least gives you something to giggle over! Essentially, like most things in this book, the ideas here are intended to be of use, promoting better understanding and a greater sense of perspective leading to change. That change may be very down to earth and practical – a new job or a different way of working; but it might also be a change within you – a different attitude or unlearning a set of emotional responses. Here's what one STEPper has to say about the impact on his work:

I used to get terribly anxious about my work. I worried about my position in relation to others – what was my status in the workplace, was I achieving to the full? I started to think this through using one of the STEP exercises (the Wise Woman, see below), and this really helped. I've come to realize that work is important but it's not all of me, there are other important things that I do. I was allowing myself to be defined too rigidly by how I was doing at work or how I thought I was doing. I'm now much more relaxed about this. Work still gets to me but I'm usually able to respond with a greater sense of distance – I don't allow it to overwhelm me.

How and when to use the ideas

So you're busy, we know that. You haven't time to stop and think. Good! Neither have we. The whole point of these exercises is that you can fit most of them into the odd corners of the day – close your

STEP BACK

eyes on a train journey – even stuck in a Tube, think things th
while driving (suggest not closing eyes on this one), ironing (ditto),
walking the dog, dropping off to sleep . . . (okay, you can close your
eyes now!).

Changing focus – stilling

It's very important to find a few minutes each day that you use for
yourself, and not feel guilty about. As we say above, this can be on a
train or other odd corner of the day, but if you can find some spaces
and time at home, start by turning off your 'phone, make yourself
comfortable and then close your eyes. Imagine you are going deep
down into yourself; what colour is it in there? What amazing little
spot-things can you see?

- Look, don't pass these things by.
- Go further down, and when you've arrived, give the thoughts that
  are still coming at you a quick look. Deal with the silly issues that
  will assail you, and then relax.
- Start by relaxing your face, and that may be as far as you get;
  check you're not slightly frowning, which is how many of us are
  when we're not thinking about it and that's not relaxed, it's
  slightly frowning!
- Let your emotions and mind drift, and you may well find that time
  has passed you by in your semi-conscious state.
- If you have more time and space, put on some gentle music and
  either lie on the floor or sit in a comfortable and supportive chair
  (how many committees could do with one of those!), and go
  through your body, relaxing each joint and limb as you get there.
- Some people like to start with the feet and work up; you may like
  to go the other way. Don't rush; it's often worth doing the whole
  thing twice to make sure you've really engaged.
- Let your mind drift once you are relaxed, and enjoy feeling the
  stress run out of you.
- You may find lighting a candle, especially a scented one, helpful.
  If you find it hard to stop your thoughts when your eyes are
  closed, keep them open and just watch the flame. The important
  thing is that this is your time; use it as you wish.
- Don't ignore the coming back process. You may need to set an

73

alarm to tell you that time's up, and you must re-engage your mind and body slowly. Sit up, re-orientate yourself, and then move slowly at first. You've been away – make sure you come back gently.

- For some, exercise is the best way to return. They like to get out in the air and walk, or cycle. Swimming is a wonderful way to chew the cud mentally – Ronni writes her best sermons in a pool ... and exercise has the added bonus of engaging those calories too.

Don't let yourself have those amazing tongue-lashing sessions in your mind where you obliterate someone you're finding hard – you know you won't do it, and you wouldn't want to either! Such fantasies don't benefit your soul or your blood pressure! (see Someone else's shoes, page 82).

If you really can't find five minutes a day, ask yourself:

- Do I need to cook every night – why not buy a TV dinner just once a week?
- Does my ironing have to be perfect? Can I afford to employ someone to do it or not do it all – is a crease a sin?
- Who else will benefit from my being more relaxed? Isn't it worth it for them, if not for me?
- Am I avoiding this 'me time' for a specific reason? What is it that I don't want time to consider?

The following are some specific STEP exercises, mostly to be employed after a relaxation session (or in the middle, before you 'come back') as above.

The Wise Woman

Make regular visits to an imaginary figure who represents wisdom. This could be a wise woman or man, or perhaps some kind of oracle. Dream up who you want it to be and where the wise one lives – the environment in which you meet. Here's one person's version, which seems to be fairly typical:

When I was struggling with my conventional faith, I started visiting the Wise Woman while walking our neighbour's dog. It's not very original, I'm afraid. She lives in a hut in the wood, she's older than me and has a way of talking that picks up on what I say and throws it back at me. Something of a mother or grandmother figure, I guess. I soon found that I could bring other things to the Wise Woman, not just my faith issues, and it really helped me to think through some job problems.

In this form of meditation, the thinker knows that he or she is really talking to himself or herself but the imaginary dialogue helps them to see the issue in a more rounded way. The role of Wise One is a reflective, balancing one. The meditator above wrote down an example, trying to recall how the start of the conversation went:

Wise W.	Hello, it's been a while.
Med.	I know, I've been busy.
Wise W.	You should never be too busy to talk . . . and think.
Med.	Well, I have a difficulty.
Wise W.	With work?
Med.	Right.
Wise W.	You're worried about the new boss not understanding your need for flexibility on Mondays and Thursdays.
Med.	I am.
Wise W.	Or is it bigger than that?
Med.	How do you mean?
Wise W.	Think back. You always get edgy when change is coming, it's natural. So maybe this is just part of a more general worry about the future at work.
Med.	I think so actually, yes.

The conversation continued for quite a bit but the meditator is adamant that thinking about things in this way brought the larger issue to the surface much more quickly. He says that the 'Wise Woman' helped him to see his fears as part of a pattern and that this enabled him to cope with them objectively rather than simply responding.

STEP BACK

High flight

This is a form of meditation that helps you to see issues objectively and to explore how they relate to one another. You'll need to be relaxed and ready to go on an imaginative journey.

Imagine that you're high above a landscape. Picture the scene, making up your own setting. At one end there's a hill or other landscape feature such as a stream or a beach. This represents where you want to get to – a more flexible lifestyle or a better job, for example.

At the other end, you can see yourself. High above, you look down on yourself – what do you see? How are you represented? You might see your physical self, much as you would if you were really flying overhead. Or you might be represented in a more allegorical form, or perhaps you see an idealised version of yourself. You might choose to be represented by an animal, perhaps a cheetah – you're fast moving and fleet of foot; or a snake – you'll keep a low profile as you travel; or you could be a tortoise – as in the fable, you'll get there in the end without any histrionics. You're not stuck with this version of yourself – an important point about this exercise is that you can change things as you go along.

Now place barriers between yourself and where you want to be. Name the barriers and represent them in your mind picture. Some examples are:

- lack of ambition – a straggly hedge that grows all over the place, blocking your path;
- too many things to do – fast-growing plants that spring up and block your way;
- an unsympathetic boss – a dangerous and scornful creature that patrols the area;

. . . and so on. Set up your mind picture in the most appropriate way for you. It doesn't have to be an earthly landscape; it could be in space as you dodge asteroids on your way to a perfect planet; it could be a totally imaginary otherworldly scene.

Take your time and come back to the scene on several occasions if necessary. Just a few minutes a day on the train would be fine, for example.

When you have something that you're satisfied with, move on to the next phase and begin to fly around the scene – as if you are a god or playwright looking down on your creation and 'yourself' in it. You're completely free to fly where you want – the people and things in the scene can't see you. What do you want to take a look at? Perhaps start with those things that are blocking your progress. Fly around them, examine them, and get to know them. Are they really as powerful as they seem? Which is actually the biggest barrier to change? As you think more about the obstacles, allow their characteristics to change in response to your ideas. For example, if your boss's attitude becomes less significant as you think about it, watch his or her representation shrink in size, or become more limited in range – it might actually start helping you to cut back some of the clinging plants!

This may seem a strange technique but the imaginative process of picturing aspects of your life in this way can be very powerful. In naming and picturing the obstacles you understand them better. At the very least, working out strategies to thwart them in the imaginary arena will make you feel better! At its best, this kind of exercise can help you think through actual ideas for change. Here's what one user said about this form of meditation:

I saw all the things that I had to do as shooting geysers of hot steam that could erupt at any time; I wasn't able to make any progress because of them. After a while, I got bored with this and it made me think that I wasn't being clear enough about what the geysers represented. This encouraged me to stop thinking in a vague way. I'd been thinking 'I've got too much to do, too many demands on me' without actually focusing on the individual issues. I realized, to my horror, that spending time with my son was one of the geysers. I'd equated this important and valuable time with things like shopping and doing the accounts. The exercise led to a reappraisal of what was really important in my life. I pictured myself turning from a frightened rabbit, jumping around dodging geysers, into a truffle-hunting wild boar seeking out the very best in life and prepared to take time over it. This didn't change my real world overnight but it calmed me down and gave me some important perspectives.

Come back to the scene from time to time. See if events in the real world have moved you any nearer to your goal. Or has your goal changed? You might want to spend some time examining your hill, stream or beach. What do they really represent? Can you add detail to bring your ideas more into focus?

I wish I'd spent more time . . .

. . . at the office?

You're on your deathbed after a long, healthy and interesting life. As you look back what are you proudest of, and what do you regret? Think back to yourself at the age you are now. For clarity, this is you in old age looking back to you at age . . . (fill in your current age):

- What does your dying self regret about this time in your life?
- What does your dying self celebrate about this time in your life?
- What could you do now to please your 'deathbed old self'?

One meditator answered this last one with, 'Find an elixir of life'!

Three things

This is a good meditation to do before you go to sleep each night. Begin by relaxing as suggested above. Then, night by night, think back over the day just passed. Find three different things to think about:

- something you'd like to have done differently;
- something you enjoyed;
- something to celebrate that's typically 'you'.

Here's an example:

- something you'd like to have done differently:
  I wish I hadn't lost my temper with Louise.
- something you enjoyed:
  I enjoyed going for a walk with my wife.
- something to celebrate that's typically 'you':
  I spent time playing Lego with Alex and became completely engrossed.

After a few days, go back over the things you chose each night (you might need to write them down). Is there a pattern emerging? Do your choices tell you things about the balance of your life? Do they suggest changes you need to make?

STEP BACK

Tracking emotions

As mentioned elsewhere in this book, the ups and downs of our emotional life can have a bearing on how we respond to issues. Feelings can be a powerful guide to where we are in our work–life balance story, but there are times when as well as experiencing feelings, we need to step aside and examine what we're going through and why.

One way of doing this is to track emotions – write down at the end of the day what your emotional state has been during the day. You could set up a simple scoring system using key emotions such as happiness, feeling low, calm, angry. You could plot these on a graph if you're mathematically minded, or set up a spreadsheet (don't be judgemental – each to their own!), or you might choose to invent a colour-coded system.

After a week or so, look back at your recorded emotions:

- Do they tell you anything about yourself?
- Are particular emotions linked to specific times of the day or week?
- Do they relate to certain events, perhaps at work? (Monday morning being an obvious one for many people, although in the new world of work Mondays won't exist in the same way.)
- Are there things you could change as a response to tracking and understanding your emotions better?

Journaling

Journaling has become a bit of a buzz word among those of us who go in for 'spiritual direction'. If that's not a term you've heard before, it's a relationship that an individual has with another, who acts as guide/mentor/friend along the spiritual journey. How this relationship works out varies from person to person, but journaling can be used by all of us, and to good effect.

It's really a form of intimate diary. First of all, you commit to undertake the discipline of writing your journal, as and when is best for you. Perhaps once a week, perhaps every evening, each of us to their own. But when you do journal, it's a detailed look back over that period of time, asking how you were feeling when various things were going on; an objective assessment of whether you

79

responded positively or not, whether that activity was good or bad for you, and how it could have been better. What were your feelings towards Jan as she tipped red wine down your shirt, or towards Esme when she congratulated you on the quality of your work yesterday? What happened? How did you react? How did you feel at the time? How do you feel now?

Then hold on for a moment; at this point people of faith would apply the question, 'What is God saying to me through this?' You may simply rephrase that as 'what can I learn through this?' It's not as easy as it sounds – it is time-consuming yet very rewarding.

Ronni's experience of journaling included the amazing sense of getting back inside her head, her emotions, months after a particularly powerful event. With hindsight, you can see whether your rage was justified, or your joy. It can be a salutary experience, a humbling method of growing. Or, it can help you to decide that yes, maybe it is time to change your job – things aren't improving or developing as you thought they would.

Ronni journals via a computer, as she finds this quicker, and it has a spell checker! You need to do this for a good period of time or you won't get the sense of perspective and growth; and of course, it's wonderful to revisit years later and really see how life has changed.

Three doors

This is a method of thinking about what you want to achieve. Imagine that there are three doors in front of you. On the first door is a sign saying 'The Imagination room'; the second door is to 'The Practical room'; and the third door leads to 'The First-step room'.

Bring your question, problem or issue to each room in turn. Let's take an example: let's say that you want to think about where your work–life story will take you in five years' time. Open the door to the first room and enter. What do you see? Perhaps you don't see much at first so begin to think about the issue, to dream and imagine where you would like to be, love to be, in five years' time. Are there things in the room that help you – perhaps an impressive desk and office equipment if you're dreaming about a senior post in an organization? Perhaps you see recording equipment or writing materials, awards, photographs of children, a wedding, a racing car . . . What do *you* see?

Look out of the window – what's the view, a Caribbean island perhaps or a dance studio or . . . ? Let your imagination run wild as you find out what and who and where you want to be. Allow your thoughts to be less prosaic if that helps – perhaps you see an abstract picture representing a healthy work–life balance.

Enjoy your time in the first room, and take a clear picture away from it as you enter the second room. Take a look at what it says on the door – 'The Practical room'.

As you enter this room, think through what you found in the first room, from a practical perspective. Don't be negative, telling yourself that it's all moonshine, just bring your practical experience and understanding to bear. Don't allow the dream of the imagination room die, but see it from a different perspective.

Let's say that you clearly identified that you'd like to have written a novel in five years' time. The purpose of the practical room is not to say, 'Don't be ridiculous, you can't do that'; rather, it is to help you think it through in practical terms with thoughts such as:

- Writing a novel is a big undertaking, you'll need to organize your ideas.
- You're going to set aside time to do this.
- You'll need some advice on the practicalities where could you go to get it?
- Do you need to share your ideas with someone you trust – get a second opinion.

Look around the room – what do you see that will help you to think about these issues – a calendar perhaps, a diary with spaces blocked out marked 'writing time'? If you feel yourself becoming discouraged by the practicalities, go back to the imagination room and refresh your dream batteries.

When you've spent time in the first two rooms you should be enthused and realistic about what you want to do. Now enter the third room, the one with 'The First-step room' on the door.

It's pretty obvious what happens in here. It's the room where you're very focused, you have one decision to make – what will be my first step to making what I saw in the first room a reality? What do you see in here, what practical options are open to you? Perhaps there's a phone number of a friend you should talk to, or a computer screen with 'Plot outline' and then a lot of space. Whatever you see in this First-step room, it should be something that you can actually achieve, a step that you can take, now.

Come back to the rooms over time and see how they change as your ambitions develop into reality – your aims and dreams will change too, of course. There might even be times when you cover the furniture in the rooms with dust sheets while you put plans on hold. You might shrink or grow particular rooms as time goes by.

Using the rooms will keep you focused on what you want to do and, wherever you are in achieving your dreams, there will always be a first step to making the next phase happen, so keep revisiting that room.

Someone else's shoes

If there's a particular person or group of people that your thoughts keep returning to, why not have a go at being them? Once you're relaxed, imagine that you are that person. Go through your body, part by part, adjusting how you sit or lie, adopting the other person's physicality.

Then imagine that person in a specific situation. Can you begin to understand them and find out what makes them tick? In your mind, go over an incident involving you both, but be the other person; see how and why they react to you in the way they do.

Try applying your new understanding the next time you meet this person.

In specific work–life balance scenarios, you might employ this technique in advance of discussing new arrangements with your boss, or to help you understand the effect of some proposed change on your family or work colleagues.

Write a meditation

As you become adept at using STEP techniques and begin to develop your own versions, why not write down some meditations? You could start with a written record of where your imaginary journeys have taken you and then begin to shape your work in a more formal sense. The advantage of this is that your focus shifts from looking inward to examining, shaping and understanding the material. You'll gain greater insight through this creative and artistic process. It doesn't need to be brilliant literature, just write something that records where you are now and where you want to be. In fact this might be a good starting point – the tension created by your aspirations and current reality. There'll be a sense of dynamic balance there, which is where we came in! So we'll go out with a sample meditation:

Change
Balance
Movement through time
Balancing who I am with where I am
Changing who we will be.

I thought I knew what I wanted
But when I got it . . .
Of course it wasn't what it was meant to be.

Step back
Be prepared to change
To change my mind
To grow my hopes
To dream
To take the first step
The first step toward change
Within me
Between us
Around us

I seek balance within, between, around, as I take that first step . . .